THE TERRORISTS:

Youth, Biker and Prison Violence

by

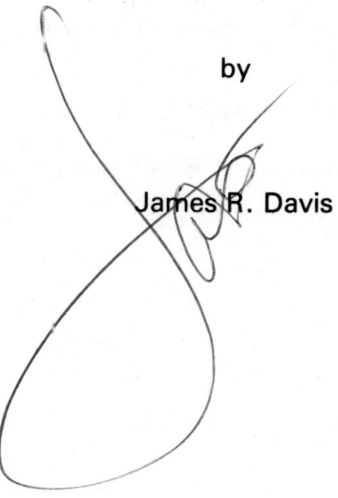

James R. Davis

DAN COR PRESS

2387 Rippey Ct.   **El Cajon, CA 92020**

Copyright © 1978 by James R. Davis. All rights reserved.
No part of this publication may be reproduced, stored in a
retrieval system, or transmitted, in any form or by any
means, electronic, mechanical, photocopying, recording,
or otherwise, without prior written permission of the
author and publisher. Manufactured in the United States
of America.

ISBN 0-89543-013-4

Library of Congress Catalog Card Number: 78-354

ACKNOWLEDGEMENTS

I would like to thank the following people, whose time, assistance and friendship have helped make this book a reality: Commander Jesse Brewer, Los Angeles Police Department; John Duffy, Sheriff, San Diego County; Edwin Miller, District Attorney, San Diego County; J L. Duchnick, Deputy District Attorney, San Diego County; Brian Cash, Parole Agent, California Adult Authority; Joel Taylor, California Department of Justice, and members of the Office of Special Investigations, San Diego County Sheriff's Office, with whom I had the privilege of working. I would like to thank the Police Departments of San Diego, Chicago and New York for allowing me to ride with them and evaluate their procedures and field practices regarding street gangs. I also wish to acknowledge my colleagues at National University for their patience and good humor.

Any author is only as good as his editors, therefore my special thanks to Jay Farris and Ellen Squire. For the past seven years, from thinking about this effort to its completion, my wife Cecelia has been both tolerant and inspirational. Thanks, Cecelia.

*"Terrorism is a tactic or technique by means of which a violent act or the threat thereof is used for the prime purpose of creating overwhelming fear for coercive purposes . . ."**

*National Advisory Committee on Criminal Justice Standards and Goals. *Report of the Task Force on Disorders and Terrorism* Page 3.

FOREWORD

The time has arrived when the general public must join with their law enforcement agencies to wage an all-out effort to eradicate the threat of terrorist violence from our society. Our country recently celebrated its bicentennial. The U.S. Constitution still stands as a model of excellence for the entire world. However, it is time to secure the freedoms guaranteed by that constitution for all our citizens; to be specific, the potential victims of terrorism.

I have devoted my professional career to the maintenance of order and the control of crime in society. Though my efforts have been well rewarded, I still see much that needs to be done.

It is intolerable that anyone need be afraid to walk the streets because of the potential of becoming a victim of gang violence. It is equally intolerable that our prisons serve as universities of crime and perversion rather than the deterrent tool for which they were established.

This book by James Davis will open the eyes of the public to the insidious social problem that terrorism engenders in our society. His descriptions of prison gang violence and outlaw biker behavior are both startlingly frank and timely.

I join with James in his plea to the American public to recognize the problem and work with their criminal justice system to eradicate and prevent a recurrence of that problem. This book opens the public's eyes. Half of the battle is won. We do not have to live in fear. It is up to you.

Captain Jesse Brewer
Commanding Officer
Los Angeles Police Department
Training Academy

TABLE OF CONTENTS

INTRODUCTION

Juvenile Commits Suicide in County Jail After Being Sodomized.

Bikers Take-over California Town—Citizens in Fear for Lives.

Suburban Crime Rates Soar—Sheriff Releases New Statistics.

"Our Television Station Has More Violence, Bloodshed and Gore Than All of Our Competitors: Please Stayed Tuned."

These headlines are indicative of an insidious sickness that permeates our society. *Violence and terrorism have become an American way of life.* We abhor the perverted rape of our children in our jails and penal institutions, yet that violence is perpetuated by our steadfast cop-outs: "You can't fight city hall," or "The punk shouldn't have been in jail to begin with."

Society responds to outlaw motorcycle gangs with disgust if in the security of the home and is terrified if confronted by those gangs in person. But disgust and terror serve no logical end. From all indications, the outlaw bike gangs were formed after World War II and their numbers continue to grow. Again, we hear, "Well, they're Americans too, so they have a right to exist," or "What do you expect me to do, I'm just one person." Unfortunately, the deceased victims of those gangs are not in a position to mobilize society against that sick segment of the whole.

Rather than face a one-on-one challenge with violence and terrorism, Americans have moved from the congested urban centers to the sanctity of suburban bedroom communities, our 20th century Promised Land. We thought we left crime and violence behind us in the city. We didn't! Crime statistics and insurance company claims illustrate that suburbia has seen an increase of criminal activity and the malicious destruction of property. The street wars of Spanish Harlem have moved to the streets in suburbia.

Why?

It is easy to come up with a glib explanation of why our penal institutions are so violent: the people who find themselves confined there are a violent lot. Outlaw motorcycle gangs spread terror because they have rejected all the values that the silent middle class hold sacred. And, crime and destruction are on the increase in suburbia because that is where the money and the people who have it reside. But these easy answers are not sufficient if the explanation is expected to assist in the eradication of violence and terrorist behavior from society. These answers just serve to initiate more questions.

Why are the more violent people in society in confinement situations? Why have outlaw motorcycle gangs rejected middle-class values? Why have monied segments of the population fled to suburbia? The questions are endless. However, if we are ever going to answer the broader question of "Why does it all happen?" we must first realize, both individually and collectively, that violence and terrorism are problematic to all of us and through a collective awareness of that problem we will be in a better position to mold public policy decisions which could limit the damage to society as a whole.

I have compiled this book of personal experiences and related readings with the objective of raising the individual's and society's conscious awareness of the problem of violence and terrorism. I have chosen, as a general focus, juvenile gangs as they relate to terrorist phenomena in society. The terrorists who murdered the Israeli Olympic teammates in Germany were at one point in history juveniles. This book will hopefully illustrate how juveniles are inducted into violence-prone peer groups which sow the seeds of violent behavior. I am not in a position to explain why some juvenile gangs are violent and some are not. Neither am I able to explain why juveniles form peer groups which may or may not develop into gangs. However, I am able to share with the reader my experiences with the more violent juvenile gangs I have encountered. Through that sharing, the reader should be in a better position to manage his home-front defenses and organize society to eradicate the problem.

Although society is made aware of violence and terrorism with frightening regularity through the entertainment and news media (as illustrated by the fourth headline at the beginning of this Introduction), it is easy to detach oneself from that violence and neutralize that awareness as "entertainment," fiction, and a media trick to sell products. The experiences I share in this book and the related reprinted articles I have included are neither censored nor fictitious. They are included to frighten the reader and give him an awareness that is not so easily dismissed. The shocking account of the rape of a juvenile in a penal institution is included to compel the reader to attempt to rectify the prison conditions within our society. It is one thing to send juveniles to jail; that issue is not germane in this book. It is indeed germane that once that juvenile is sent to prison, he or she must submit to sodomy as one of the rites of passage into prison gang membership.

I have sectioned this book into four general areas or parts: I. RITES OF PASSAGE; II. THE NATURE OF GANG TERRORISM AND THE ACTORS; III. WEAPONS AND ARTIFACTS; and IV. EXPECTATIONS AND PROGNOSIS. The first part, as the title indicates, relates how juveniles in prisons must submit to sodomy as an initiation into prison gangs and how outlaw motorcycle bikers initiate new members into their gangs. The rites through which an individual passes to gain membership are designed to destroy the initiate's old identity and indelibly impress on him that he is "now of the gang." The second part discusses the terrorist act in general and describes those who perpetrate those acts against society. The reprinted articles further delineate the specific identities of the more violent actors and suggest some possible preventative measures designed to reduce acted-out behavior patterns. The third section describes the "tools of the trade" of the terrorist. The use of drugs, firearms and bombs serves to herald the entrance of the terrorist into the society at large. Awareness of the tools they use will allow society to plan counter attacks and initiate preventative measures to reduce the media's attention, which the terrorist group so desperately needs in order to function. The article by Peretti, Carter and McClinton discusses how society can read the graffiti in the juvenile's restroom and find clues to his predispositions and his future targets. By studying these clues society might find a way to reduce the tensions and frustrations which may lead to terrorist acts in adult life.

The fourth part, EXPECTATIONS AND PROGNOSIS, is a reprint from the *Report of the Task Force on Disorders and Terrorism* published by the U.S. Department of Justice in 1976. It serves to illustrate that the federal government is cognizant of the terrorist problem in society and indicates that if the problem is ever to be solved a cohesive national effort must be undertaken.

As a whole, the book is pessimistic in its portrayal of terrorist phenomena. The graphic rape of Mark in the first segment of Part I is not meant to excite the prurient interests of the reader. Rather it starkly and realistically describes the prison rite of passage as a means of inciting society to reasoned action designed to remedy the problems found in jails and penal institutions. The disgusting rituals of the outlaw bikers are not half as bad in print as they are to the initiate and to the author, when I witnessed them. Prisons can be improved by eradicating the conditions which perpetuate institutional violence. The outlaw biker gangs can be persuaded or coerced into avoiding a specific locality. That requires total community support of the criminal justice agencies within the locality. All citizens must work toward that end.

In publishing this book I hope to make the general public aware of the problems of violence and terrorism in society generally and in the reader's community specifically. This awareness should spur a concerned citizenry to collective social action. The undesirable social conditions which lead to terrorism and violence can be ameliorated only through legislation and education. My half of this task is completed when this book hits the bookstore. It is now in your hands to take this information and do something with it.

James R. Davis

PART I

RITES OF PASSAGE

Rites of passage may be defined as ceremonial acts or a series of acts which move the individual from one place to another, either physically or mentally. The following sub-chapters illustrate two rituals through which an individual might have to pass on his or her way to gang membership. The rituals are similar in their impact on the initiates; they either pass the tests and are assimilated into the gang or they fail their test and are rejected by their peers.

These rites of passage into prison gangs, motorcycle clubs, and street gangs in general may encompass many different modalities. I have chosen to feature the rites that I became familiar with when I worked as an undercover law enforcement officer.

"An Invitation To A Fly Race" is included here as a stark example of the violence inherent in our prisons and juvenile institutions. My academic colleagues will find it an insignificant incident in the scientific study of crime and criminals. My former law enforcement officer colleagues will think of me as a "bleeding liberal" to have even written the piece, let alone publish it. However, regardless of the criticism, it is included as a vivid example of the depravity to which some members of our society have sunk.

Much of the descriptive material and dialogue is very frank. It is not included to stimulate the more prurient interests of the reader. Rather, the frankness should serve to open the eyes of the reader to a very serious social problem — the literal and figurative rape of many young people who find themselves in the American "Gulag."

I do not attempt to justify the rightness or wrongness of the general incarceration of criminals. That effort would entail many additional volumes. I am concerned, however, with the violence inherent within our prisons. To send any person into confinement is one thing. For that person to be gang-raped and perverted is another. Therefore, I feel it necessary to relate those incidents which culminated in the "death" of an adolescent male called Mark. Mark (and all those like him) is not a figment of my imagination. He is the boy-next-door gone to jail. He is a distillation of many young men I have known. Although this is therefore fiction, the events and principles written about do occur. I have talked with prison officials, inmates and their families and feel confident that this story is an accurate reflection of prison life.

"Outlaws on Wheels" presents a more academic or scientific treatment of gang terrorism and initiation rites, a treatment which is sustained throughout the remainder of the book. Bikers have received considerable attention in the media recently. I am concerned, however, with the very nature and effect of that treatment. It remains more arbitrary than informative. From my past experience in the law enforcement field, I have had the opportunity to drift in and out of the bikers' world. Those experiences afford me the opportunity to share with you a glimpse into the outlaw motorcycle world. The public's fear of motorcycle gangs emanates from their ignorance of that particular segment of society. I feel assured that by sharing some of my first-hand knowledge of bikers with the public, they will be in a better position to deal with the biker phenomenon in their own life experiences.

The underlying or bottom-line principle which sustains an outlaw motorcycle gang is not unlike that which sustains any primary group. [Note: A primary group is defined as a pair, triad or small clique, organized around informal leadership, which exists to offer its member social status and cohesion and whose members have role definitions to sustain them.] Therefore, the reader should be in a better position to deal with a motorcycle gang if he is aware that they are a close-knit primary group and that their group cohesion is more significant than the behaviors they act out. That is not to say that they cannot be potentially dangerous. They are and will continue to be dangerous to society at large. To that end, my prescription to the general public is to "avoid them like the plague." Granted, that is not helpful to the individual who finds himself or herself in a one-on-one or more likely a five- or six-on-one confrontation. That individual has just struck out. He will probably become the civilian victim used in the initiation of a newer member into the gang or just the human object of the group's disdain for the values embraced by the general public.

Therefore, I entreat you to read this section with an open mind. Do not discard the book because you may be offended by the language. Take the responsibility to become an informed citizen. With that responsibility in hand, initiate public policy which will diminish the incidence of rape and violence in prisons and remove the outlaw biker problem from society. The power to effect those changes rests with the reader. It is up to you.

AN INVITATION TO A FLY RACE

The work day had come to an end at last. The maximum security institution was gearing down for another peaceful evening. The four o'clock count, which assured the administration that all bodies were accounted for, had tallied with the official figures in the Superintendent's office. The next count would be at midnight. The chow line had dwindled to only a few, with the bulk of the inmate population on "free-time" recreation. Behind the chow line lay the overcooked food that had begun to cool and congeal inside the stainless steel pans which had once rested over cauldrons of boiling hot water. The three offenders assigned to serve chow took time out for a smoke break and rap session which revolved around the subjects of sex, liquor, drugs or a recent fight. Two of the cooks alternated drags on a joint laced with "angel dust," while the third looked around sharply before shoveling a handful of reds into his mouth. He chased them with warm "pruno"—jailhouse lingo for booze made from fermented prunes. The guys did not have to be too concerned about being caught; they were back by the old walk-in freezer in the rear of the kitchen. The new freezer which housed the desired items of prison barter—prunes, sugar, and meat—was up front and was only opened by the chief civilian cook. The old freezer housed only the undesired perishables—flour, wheat and rice—and thus was a safe place for the kitchen inmates to gather. The kitchen cons were also relatively safe from any official harassment, as their families supplied them with lots of money. The head civilian cook needed some of their money to keep the alcohol level in his blood high enough to allow him to work eight hours a day in the juvenile jungle.

The oldest, and by that virtue, head inmate cook, shuffled over to the others behind the old freezer. When they saw him, they recognized that familiar hungry look in his eyes. He mumbled, "A good night for a fly race, don't you think?" The three inmates rubbed their crotches and began to laugh. "All right, man!" "Right on, mother fucker!" "Who we gonna plug tonight, that new queen?" The head cook knew who "that new queen" was and he had already set in motion the events that would bring the "queen" to him rather than require he or the other gang members going to him. Yes, the Daggers, the kitchen prison gang, were organized.

The Daggers ran the kitchen. Other gangs ran other departments. The entire prison was run by gangs of inmates like the Daggers. They ran the offices with only nominal supervision by the civilian supervisors. Guards were usually few in number, rarely if ever exceeding the ratio of one guard to every three inmates. Any warden or superintendent who did not agree that the inmates ran their joint or institution, did so either from fear of losing his job or out of ignorance or just to make his institution seem tight. The fact of the matter was, inmates controlled this youth institution solidly, although they normally did not oppose the civilian authorities. The Daggers would not enter into conflict with the civilian supervisor of the kitchen.

These rules apply to most prisons. Rarely does an inmate gang come into conflict with the guards or supervisors (although incidents like Attica do illustrate the exception to this rule). Inmates gang together to defend themselves from the other gangs. Whether one is a member of a gang becomes not a choice of preference, but one of survival! A biker might affiliate with the "Bravos," "Aryan Brotherhood," "Outlaws," or "Choppers." The ethnic minorities affiliate with the "Persuasions," "White Polar Bears," "Stylistics," "Crips," "Mexican Mafia," or the "Black Panthers." Each group exists to protect its members. A loner is often the prey of any group until he joins a gang and even then he might become a victim of predators within his chosen gang as a sort of initiation or pay-off for being allowed to join.

The Daggers' pigeon, or object of the planned homosexual attack, had already been selected and the steps necessary to arrange for his being in the right place at the right time had already taken place. Their pigeon was a new inmate by the name of Mark. He was eighteen years old, from Concord, California and was starting a two-year sentence for selling a "lid," or ounce of marijuana, to an undercover officer. He came from a successful middle-class family in the suburbs. His father made thirty thousand dollars a year and his mother popped pills and chased them with Beefeaters. They thought it wise for Mark, the oldest of four boys, to go to the local junior college for a couple of years. He had above average intelligence and was on the high school and junior college swimming teams. The judge who sentenced him to jail did so as a deterrent to the other youths on California's college campuses, even though it was only Mark's second encounter with the law. He had once been arrested as a minor, for possession of alcohol.

Mark was transported from his local county jail to the youth authority institution. He was not alone. There were four other juveniles being taken to the joint with him. All had spent some time in jails and been released on probation. Mark was the only exception; he had never really been in serious trouble. All five were alike in one respect; none had done time at a large institution and all were silently afraid of what was about to happen.

The prisoners were removed from the van at the prison gates and were marched across a large open field known as the *yard* to the receiving and processing building. On the way across the yard Mark got an uneasy feeling from the inmates who loitered about and whistled at them. He was the youngest and most slender of the group and received the most attention from their group of admirers. One guy started walking next to him and put his hand on Mark's buttocks before the guard yelled a warning to "keep clear!"

Mark was led into a room with waist-high tables where all five were told to strip and place all their belongings on the table. Although Mark had undressed and showered with other men before, that had been with friends in gym class or with his fellow teammates. This was different. He felt an uneasy feeling in the pit of his stomach and knew that his face was getting red. When he hesitated, one of the guards laughed and yelled, "What's the matter, kid? Never seen another guy's pecker before?" This had not helped Mark, as now the other four guys, the two receiving guards and the inmate who worked for the guards were looking at him. He pulled his shorts off and tried to stand in such a way so that the others couldn't see his penis. He needn't have worried; the inmate orderly was not interested in Mark's penis, but his lean white ass. The orderly was a member of the Daggers and was placed in receiving so that the gang could have the "choice morsels" as they entered the institution.

The guard who seemed to be in charge yelled to the five to stand in line, front to back. The four quickly lined up behind Mark. They were marched to a barber chair. Mark was told to sit in the chair. It was cold against his naked ass but he was no longer overly concerned with his nakedness. What was of concern was his fear of what was about to happen to him. The guard nodded to the inmate, who then picked up an electric razor and shaved Mark's head. He was skinned. When all five had been shorn like sheep in the spring, they were marched into another room where they were greeted by a man in a white coat who seemed to be a doctor. He told

Mark to open his mouth and then felt around his mouth with an ungloved hand. He then told Mark to lift his testicles so he could be sure Mark had not concealed anything down there that was forbidden in the institution. Then the doctor turned Mark around and told him to bend over and spread his cheeks. Mark suddenly felt a sharp pain and yelled, "What the FUCK?" just as the doctor removed his finger from Mark's anus. The two guards moved over to the examination area and the doctor replied, "I had to make sure you weren't a twentieth century Papillon. We read and go to the movies, too." Mark stood up, his ass still smarting from the examination and he moved out of the way.

When all five had been thoroughly examined, the guards herded them over to a showering area. They were told to wash with the lye soap provided by the institution. The lye soap, they were told, was to prevent the introduction of infectious skin diseases into the institution. As they were showering, one inmate had whispered to Mark, "I can't wait to shower with you when no guards are watching. You better not drop the soap or what the Doc just did will be kid's stuff." Mark tried to ignore him and hurried to rinse the strong soap from his body.

After the shower, they were given baggy shirts and trousers and were told to put them on, even though they had no towels with which to dry off. Although Mark had a thirty-inch waist, the inmate orderly gave him a size twenty-six pair of pants. He could barely button the pants and he again felt his face redden as he realized his pants were molded to his skin and everything he had, showed. He thought he saw the inmate clerk wink at him but realized that he must have imagined it. Mark was not imagining the wink; the orderly belonged to the Daggers.

The five were herded into a dormitory-like room. The room was filled with beds; there must have been two hundred. They were told which one they had been assigned and that this was only temporary until they saw the institution counselor. The five were given a sheet and a blanket and told to make their cots. When they had finished, they could go out onto the yard until count at four p.m. To be counted, they were informed, they had to be sitting on their beds.

Mark went out to the yard. He was getting over being embarrassed by his too-tight pants, but he still received the attention of several inmates when he passed them. He thought if he could only have a cigarette, things would at least seem better. He had brought a carton with him from the jail but it and all his personal effects had been confiscated in receiving.

Mark was standing alone in the yard when a large, heavy-bearded, older guy walked up to him and said, "Hi, new here? Don't let those assholes pat your ass, kid, unless you want to get corn-holed."

Mark felt his face get beet-red. He started to walk away and then stopped. Turning, he yelled, "Hey man, fuck off."

"Hey, wait a minute. I'm just trying to help you. If you think you can stay cherry in here through the night, good luck. Fuck you, faggot."

As the older guy started to leave, Mark realized he had made a serious mistake. "Wait, I'm sorry. I'm new here and frankly scared shitless. I'm really sorry."

"Hey, okay. I know what it's like; I was new here once myself. My name's Jeremy, what's yours?"

"I'm Mark. You got a cigarette? I'm about to die."

"Sure, take what's left of the pack, but be careful of accepting things from other inmates. It can get you into a lot of trouble. There's the noon lunch whistle. See you on the yard after lunch."

Mark asked some inmates where chow was being served and made his way inside. As he passed through the food line, the guy dishing out the meat loaf looked at Mark and added another portion. The guard was looking away and Mark said thanks. The cook just smiled. Mark ate quickly, stacked his tray near the garbage cans and went back out on the yard. He reached for the cigarettes, then saw Jeremy had left him only one. "Well, don't look a gift horse in the mouth," he thought.

Soon Jeremy returned and sat next to Mark. They were sitting in a corner of the yard, as alone as they would ever be in prison. "You know, kid, in this place you gotta have friends, you gotta be a member of a gang. I'm going to be your friend and I'll see if I can get you into my gang, the Daggers. We run this fucking joint."

Mark was cautious. He had seen enough movies about prison to be wary. Mark thought it over and realized that he was very much alone and the idea of a friend and other guys to pal around with would help him get through his two-year sentence.

"Do you think they'll take me? I feel awfully alone and I sure would like to have you as a friend."

"Well, all I can do is ask. I'll let you know. Since we're friends, I brought you a carton of smokes. It's just a loan until you can get some to repay me."

Mark was on the verge of tears; he was so afraid and this guy was going to help him make it. "Thanks, I sure can use those. I'm out. I know I shouldn't smoke . . . you know, it's bad for my swimming . . . but all rules exist to be broken. Anyway, I didn't see a pool on my way in here so I don't have to worry about keeping in shape. I'll pay you as soon as my parents send me some money. Thanks again."

"Think nothing of it, kid. I've got to go now and get to work in the kitchen."

"So long, Jeremy, and thanks again," replied Mark as Jeremy walked away.

Mark had nothing to do until four when he had to be at his bunk for count. He sat in the yard smoking one cigarette after another. He had carelessly forgotten to hide the carton of cigarettes under his shirt. A big guy came over and squatted right in front of Mark. He must have weighed two hundred and fifty pounds and not one ounce of it was fat. The way he was squatting, Mark could just see something sticking out of the top of his boot. The guy checked for any guards in the area, lifted the knife he had hidden in his boot, and looked Mark directly in the eyes. With his free hand, he picked up Mark's cigarettes. "Thanks for the smokes kid, and if you say anything, I'll kill ya."

Mark didn't say a word and the guy stood up and walked away. Mark thought, "Oh well, next time I'll take them to my bunk; they'll be safer there. I was stupid for leaving them lying out, just asking to be taken. I'll know better next time."

Moments later, Jeremy came up to Mark. "Hey Mark, let me have the smokes back. I forgot I owe the inmate cook a carton. If I don't pay up I'll be in a lot of trouble."

Mark stammered, "Jeremy, some dude took them. He pulled a knife on me and just took your cigarettes."

Jeremy looked angry and snapped, "I don't give a fuck what happened, you get me a carton by supper or you've had it. Do you understand?"

Jeremy had already laid claim to Mark as the Daggers' new pigeon and had spread the word that no smokes were to go to the new guy with the "tight ass." It was common knowledge that Jeremy worked for the head cook, who was the leader of the Daggers. And nobody crossed the Daggers. Mark tried to get a carton of cigarettes from everyone he saw. But the word was out and he returned to his bunk, just before count, still owing Jeremy a carton of smokes. When the count was cleared, all the inmates converged on the dining room. Mark made it through the line and again got an extra portion of meat from the friendly cook. He sat at an empty table and felt uneasy because no one joined him.

Before he finished his supper, Jeremy came out of the kitchen, dressed in his kitchen whites, and sat next to Mark.

"You got my smokes, kid?"

"No, Jeremy, but I'll try after chow."

"Well, I know you'll come through . . . Oh, by the way, have you ever been invited to a fly race? We have them and bet on the winners. Maybe you could win the race and pay me back the cigarettes."

Mark was confused, but at the same time saw a ray of hope. "No, I've never been to a fly race, but if it'll keep you out of trouble, I'll try to win a carton to pay you with."

Jeremy smiled and replied, "Okay, kid, come with me into the kitchen. Chow's almost over and I saw the head inmate and a couple of other cooks back by the old freezer. I think they're going to have a race."

Mark followed Jeremy through the kitchen door. They wound their way back to where five other inmates, all in cooks' whites, were standing around. Jeremy introduced

Mark to the cook who had given him extra portions earlier. The cook asked, "Do you know how to play?" Mark replied he didn't but was willing to learn. The cook continued, "Okay, here's what you do. Go over to the garbage cans, grab a fly and tear off his wings so he can't fly. See, like the one I have here in my hand."

Mark went over to the garbage area and was finally able to catch a fly. He returned to the group and managed to pull the wings off the fly though his hand shook with indecision.

"Okay, kid," the cook continued, "let's get inside the old freezer; the cold makes the race more fun." The six inmates entered the freezer, looking around to make sure no one saw them enter. It was cold inside, just cold enough to keep the weevils from hatching and somewhat numb the flies.

The cook now turned to Mark, "Now, I understand that you owe Jeremy a carton of cigarettes. I propose that we race our flies for one carton. If you win, I'll pay Jeremy the carton you owe him. If you lose, you'll owe both of us a carton. Sound fair?" Mark nodded his head. The cook continued, "Now, let's put our flies down on the floor and the first one to cross that red line wins."

Mark and the cook put their flies on the floor and stood up. Mark cheered his fly like his friends did him when he was swimming. All of a sudden, the cook stepped over and smashed Mark's fly under his boot. Mark started to yell, but two of the other cooks grabbed his arms and one stuffed a towel into his mouth. He was very confused and afraid. The same insulation which kept the freezer cold would also keep his screams, if he could scream, from being heard. The cook looked at Mark and smiled, "Hey, you lose, fucker!" Mark was terrified. He knew that the guards would not know that he was missing until after their midnight count. Further, the inmate cooks wouldn't bring him here if there was any real chance of their being disturbed. His situation seemed hopeless.

The head cook turned to the two inmates holding Mark's arms and said, "Tie him over that sack of wheat with his ass high up; I don't like to have to bend over too much." Mark was pulled face down over the sack of wheat. His hands were tied securely to the pallet upon which the sack of wheat sat. The gag in his mouth was removed; his screams could not have been heard anyway. He knew he could kick his attackers but he hated to think how they would retaliate. He heard the head cook command Jeremy, "You get him ready and I'll go first, then you, since you got him here, and then the other guys." Jeremy could hardly speak, but managed an "Okay, boss."

Jeremy, with the precision of a surgeon, pulled his knife from his boot and knelt down behind Mark. He spoke very softly to Mark. "Now kid, we can be really close friends. It won't hurt as much if you relax. I know, I was once new here myself and received an invitation to this fly race. I had to hit the wheat when I first arrived and now I'm a full-fledged member of the Daggers. You just relax and you'll get over it and in no time you'll get your turn with a new pigeon. Now, don't be foolish and try to resist us. There are six of us and only one of you." Jeremy started the tip of his knife at the bottom of Mark's pant leg and proceeded to slit the material up to Mark's crotch. He repeated the process on the other leg until Mark's pant legs lay wide open. Jeremy then started to slit Mark's pants the rest of the way up to his waistline. He had trouble in not cutting into Mark's flesh because the pants fit so tightly. Finally, Mark's lean white ass was fully exposed.

Mark couldn't believe what was happening to him. Jeremy must be crazy, they all must be crazy. He tried to kick but Jeremy stuck him with the point of the knife. Mark knew that if he didn't resist, he wouldn't be hurt as much, but he couldn't get the thought out of his mind that he was being gang-raped and he had to resist in any way he could.

As soon as Jeremy had finished and Mark was prepared, the head cook moved in behind him. He unbuckled his belt and dropped his pants and shorts. He pulled Mark's legs apart and positioned himself for entry. Mark could see the other cooks had unzipped their pants and were fondling themselves with anticipation. All of a sudden he felt a blinding pain that started at his anus and consumed his entire body. Soon he could feel no specific origin of pain, just that his entire body was being raped. He was vaguely aware when the head cook grunted and then stepped back. Then he felt Jeremy enter him and heard him moaning. The repeated sexual attacks and the thirty-two degree temperature combined to allow Mark the release of unconsciousness.

He awoke in a hospital bed. The inmate orderly came over to him and said, "Hey, how you doing? We didn't know if you'd make it. Yeah, they brought you in here around 12:30 this morning, half frozen and all bloody. You sure ought to watch out hanging around that kitchen. You might just get yourself killed next time, boy."

Mark could barely mumble, but he managed to say, "No, the next time I go to the freezer, I'll be a Dagger. No, I won't be killed, I got some business to take care of there. Hey, you know how I can get a job in receiving and processing?"

OUTLAWS ON WHEELS

Terrorist groups and street gangs, most generally portrayed in articles as outlaw motorcycle gangs, are a pervasive and relentless social problem. By the same token, their maladapted behavior is very puzzling. We are not able to adequately label the actors to assist us in defining their philosophies or personality compositions. Their behaviors all differ somewhat according to the nature of and the typology of their gang. Nor can we explain away their existence with rhetorical excuses. Behavioral theories, such as mental deficiency, latent homosexuality, superego masochism, the affect of abnormal body size, or some weird state of mind whereby our actors are possessed by some demonic force, cannot explain the phenomenon. In fact, not only do most of our current theories prove unworkable in categorizing these violent and fanatical individuals, but frankly very little is really known about them.

Some theorists attribute the ganging syndrome to the need for goal achievement, while others postulate that the problem lies within the framework of our society. For example, some individuals in the society are disillusioned or feel totally rejected and, as a result, exemplify behaviors characterized by social withdrawal or anomie.

While one social critic is convinced that persons who cruise around in filthy clothing on motorcycles have grief-ego persecution complexes, other social critics suggest that gang members simply did not receive adequate guidance as youngsters. It is possible that the application of altruistic values coupled with strong parental guidance models which are reinforced by positive school experiences might have put the individual in a Volkswagen as opposed to his stripped-down Harley-Davidson motorcycle, however none of the aforementioned theories have yet to be validated.

To more fully comprehend the biker phenomenon, I chose to spend a considerable amount of time with those persons. After attending some of their meetings, visiting their homes (yes, they have homes) and associating with them in the course of their "normal day" I would like to share with you some of my observations.

As I mentioned in the introduction, many writers have discussed varying types of deviant behavior and identified group customs and values. Few have delved into life styles. Here are my findings.

A little history is in order at this point to familiarize the reader with the evolution of the motorcycle gang phenomenon. Probably the first group of outlaw bikers to be identified was on the West Coast. The group was located in San Bernardino, California. This remains a locale for a large concentration of Hell's Angels and other motorcycle gangs today. Other outlaw bikers also reside there and all may label themselves as "Berdoo" bikers as well. The first gang was named the POBOBS, an acronym meaning, "Pissed Off Bastards of Bloomington," an area near San Bernardino.

The Hell's Angels may have gotten their start in one of three different areas. Possibly, after World War II, a group of individuals banded together in the San Francisco area. Supposedly, the leader of the gang was an ex-pilot who had been affiliated with an air bomber squadron in England, which was named the Hell's Angels squadron. I have not been able to substantiate this story; however, according to the United States Air Force, a squadron by that name did exist. Another opinion has it that the Hell's Angels got their start in Los Angeles as a legitimate motorcycle club and progressively became an outlaw gang who found themselves constantly in trouble with the law. A third story claims that the Hell's Angels were an offshoot or splinter chapter of the POBOBS. Regardless of their origins, bikers have continued to be feared as a threat and menace to the general public. A number of police agencies attribute the increasing problems of vice crime (prostitution, gambling, smuggling) and narcotics in large part to the involvement of outlaw motorcycle gangs. Biker gangs have gotten involved in everything from massage parlors to trafficking illicit drugs. They own businesses which are designed to act as fronts to launder the profits gleaned from the gang's criminal activities. Their involvement in those criminal activities is relative to the overall size and organization of their gang.

The basic structure of all biker groups is somewhat similar. Each gang, depending upon its size, may have chapters. Each club chapter has a president, treasurer, sergeant-at-arms, and possibly other officers, like a publicity chairman. By-laws codify their bizarre rituals, unlawful acts, and often the initiation ceremonies which may differ radically from club to club.

Their members generally have unremarkable beginnings in terms of their motives for joining outlaw motorcycle gangs. There does not appear to be any precipitating events which lead up to gang affiliation. However, most bikers do have a history of confrontations with law enforcement agencies which usually started when they were teenagers. Their school and work experiences have generally been negative and sporadic. Their failure in school and in the work market may very well reinforce their desire to excel in criminal activities, thereby attaining the positive rewards of that activity—fame and money. In keeping with their poor work habits, many bikers lead transient lives, wandering from chapter to chapter, town to town. They commit enough crime to "get by" while associating with very few non-biker people. They frequently live in groups of no more than three or four other bikers, usually moving out of the apartment before the rent is due.

Outlaw bikers have developed a jargon and dress distinctly their own. Their language appears to be a combination of drug culture slang and terms developed to identify and distinguish their vehicular contraptions from the rest of the world. For instance, motorcycles may be called "hogs," "choppers," or "rails." Their dress is commonly referred to as trash, with or without colors. Colors distinguish the geographical locale of the member's particular gang, the name of the gang, whether the member is new to the organization or not and the types of motorcycle parts one uses or recommends. The member might also have on his T-shirt jacket or denim vest various insignia that resemble military medals, except that the insignia worn by outlaw bikers are far from honorable. Traditionally, the medals distinguish the wearer's sexual exploits. His decorations tell the world, "I'm together," which of course translates into being masculine and sexually active. Examples of that statement might range from hanging a condom on the shirt or vest to the member's flying his "wings."

Wings distinguish whether the biker's "old lady" or "mamma" or "woman" is a white chick (white wings), or a black chick (black wings), or an Oriental (yellow wings). Wings may also signify that the biker has orally copulated his chick. Wings tipped in red, or red wings, signify the female was having her menstrual cycle when orally copulated. Brown wings signify the female was anally copulated. Green signifies that the biker had intercourse with or copulated a female with a venereal disease. Purple or blue signifies intercourse or copulation with a dead female. Gold wings are very seldom seen and signify all of the aforementioned plus whatever the wearer chooses to communicate! Wings are worn predominantly on the left side of the jacket or vest.

Bikers also periodically add other ornaments which may include law enforcement badges, either taken from officers or purchased from pawn shops. Many times the words or illustration of "hands gripped together" signifies that the biker is affiliated with other gangs than his own. This affiliation is normally done for protection, usually from the Hell's Angels. "M" patches may be worn to signify marijuana is used. Often, marijuana is pinned on the jacket or vest. Letters grouped together may mean various things. M.C. may mean "Mother Chapter." B.T.R.H. usually means "Born to Raise Hell." F.T.W. means "Fuck the World." D.F.F.L. means "Dope Forever, Forever Loaded." S.T.P. means "Kill or Slay The Pig," "pig" being the bikers' derogatory term for law enforcement or police officer and should not be confused with the drug S.T.P. The reader should note that I found variations in colors, patches, or insignia used and they are usually changed often.

I also found that the worse I dressed and the more foul-mouthed I became, coupled with an appearance of knowing generally "what was happening," the more I was able to gain entrance and talk with the members on a regular basis. I discovered within any gang a hierarchy of allegiances based primarily on how tough one claimed to be. The good fighters or those that had been in state prison, usually labeled "the joint," maintained positions of leadership. Although there is often strong leadership, the gangs are socially volatile and well-planned initiations can explode into total chaos.

I found their initiations were unique in their dehumanizing and grotesque requirements, but were probably the only area of biker gang phenomena that did not differ in purpose from gang to gang, which purpose is to submerge the initiate's old identity and create a new role as a gang member. Any male who hoped to become an outlaw member was usually one who had been known to the group or at least to a few of the gang's members for some time. This requirement also held true for prospective female members.

The female's initiation usually included her being "gang-banged." That meant that she was repeatedly made to have intercourse with all or a large number of active gang members. She might also be subjected to sodomy, oral copulation, or physical torture. If she survived, she was

23

usually made a member of the gang. For the male desiring membership, a female was also involved. She was usually chosen by the initiate. That female was also gang-banged. However, the semen, blood or other body fluids were collected and poured over the biker-to-be's colors. His pants and T-shirt were normally placed under "the action," similar to the sheets on a conjugal bed. In other variations of this ritual, the gang members could defecate, urinate, vomit, spit, or pour liquids of any sort on the initiate's colors. The new member then donned his colors, which were to remain free from washing forever! The stench that seems to leap out at anyone who gets too close to a new gang member is readily understood. The initiation may also include the initiate's eating the carcass of a dead animal or parts thereof. He may also be required to consume large quantities of liquor or narcotics, or perform acts designed to shock the non-biker community.

Among their more repulsive and questionable antics, I found that they even try to "gross-out" or shock their fellow members. For example, one particular biker would catch a bird and then bite off its head, allowing the blood to trickle from his mouth as he yelled "all right!" Another member, with some baiting, would take a bite out of a maggot-infested carcass as the gang cruised down a country road. I remember one particular occasion when the biker could not lift a dead rabbit from the pavement because the thing had been cooked onto the asphalt. He was forced to lay on the ground, belly down, and tried, to no avail, to bite a piece of the hardened animal from the road. Another fellow would laugh loudly to gain his gang's attention and then eat left-over dog food which sat in a filthy dish on the back porch of one of their residences. One biker at that residence told me that the bowl was never washed and birds, squirrels and even an occasional skunk ate from the dish. Still another biker would walk into a supermarket in a small town and scream, "Want to see my peter?" Then he would take off his pants and expose himself. He might, if not satisfied with the shoppers' reactions, fondle himself and scream obscenities. When he felt he had shocked everyone sufficiently, he would leave the store. He could rest assured that he would not be arrested. He chose stores in small towns where the gang could intimidate the local law enforcement officers and where he knew that, even if arrested, no other gang member would compromise his identity.

No outlaw biker rats on another biker. This might be said to be a universal rule respected by all outlaw gangs. If you are a Raider and you witnessed an Iron Crateman commit a crime, say murder or robbery, you would not volunteer any information. This would mean saying nothing to police officers or even to rival gang members. The clasped-hands patch spoken of earlier is an example of this close-knit grouping together or inter-gang loyalty among biker gangs.

Although it may seem all they do is commit crimes, they do take time out for celebrations. They celebrate birthdays of members or celebrate upon the return from a good run; that is, a long road trip. Those parties, I can attest, can become very violent, since there is usually an abundance of weapons, drugs and orgiastic behavior.

Universal to all biker gangs is the carrying of weapons, especially on long runs and at their parties. Usually their weapons are displayed prominently on the rear rack of their hog, the sissy-bar. Their rifle or shotgun will be strapped along with a sleeping bag or bed roll. It is not a violation of California law to carry a long-barreled weapon in plain sight, so most bikers do carry those weapons. I might add here, the reader is not to be confused with arrests commonly made on charges for the carrying of concealed weapons or having loaded weapons within city limits. Those arrests have long been a point of leverage for law enforcement in dealing with bikers. However, that tool has not been a demonstrated deterrent universally, for even today most of the outlaw bikers carry weapons openly.

Outlaw motorcycle gangs seem to behave as a cohesive pack. This gang unity is emphasized by symbolic dress and the use of nicknames. Often, nicknames are used to maintain anonymity. Nicknames may also reflect a person's size or type of beard or the crime that is their specialty. Such names could be Skinny or Gordo; Fuzzy or Redbeard; Bingo, for one who commits gambling offenses; or Trasher, for an assaultive type of individual. Female members have nicknames as well, but normally have a patch on their vest or jacket stating, "Property of _____." The name of the male who considers her his property is then added. Some female members are considered the property of the entire gang.

To both male and female members, their colors and reputation have a great deal to do with the gang's inevitable survival. Not only does the reputation of a gang and its members play an important part in their day-to-day survival, but that "rep" may be the only thing that can keep a biker alive should he or she ever go to jail or prison. During the past five or six years a number of outlaw motorcycle gangs have even pledged neutrality on prison grounds. In California, for instance, bikers from rival gangs have formed a very cohesive prison gang. That gang, commonly referred to as the Aryan Brotherhood, functions primarily to protect themselves from rival prison gangs. Opposing prison groups such as the Mexican Mafia, the Black Guerrilla Family, and the Ku Klux Klan all have memberships distinctly different from bikers and war goes on back and forth among them. Literally, a biker that is not affiliated with a prison biker chapter is in danger of losing his life!

After intense review of the literature and more importantly, by traveling across the country to discuss the outlaw biker phenomenon with law enforcement authorities in major cities and small towns alike, I have come to the following conclusions about this pathetic category of people. Stay away from them. The newly initiated motorcycle gang member has passed through a dehumanizing rite of passage. His former identity is dead. His new identity is that of a "member of the pack." If he is confronted by an outsider, i.e. any of the non-biker public, he may wreak havoc on the individual out of no particular malice to that individual. His only source of an identity is from and of his gang. Anything which could diminish his group identity, i.e. any manner of confrontation with the public where he would obviously be the loser, could destroy his entire psychological existence.

For that reason he will do anything to maintain, if not enhance, his identification with his gang. He is deadly. I caution the general public from engaging in any confrontation where the biker stands a chance of losing status or his identity. Other than avoiding any confrontation with an outlaw biker, I strongly urge the general public to contact their local law enforcement authorities. Ask them how they plan to deal with an assault on their locality by a motorcycle gang. Ask them if you could assist them in ways such as contacting the town or county council to support an increased police budget. Stay away from outlaw bikers and support local law enforcement to make headlines like "Bikers Take-over California Town — Citizens in Fear for Lives" a thing of the past.

PART II

THE NATURE OF GANG TERRORISM AND THE ACTORS

The exploration of the terrorist phenomenon must encompass five distinct but interrelated areas. Part I graphically illustrated the violence inherent in gang behavior in general. In this chapter I hope to share with the reader insights into the acts and actors that are both malicious and dangerous.

I have presented my comments on the identities of the actors to expand the reader's awareness of who may potentially "do them in." Dr. Milgrim's article continues that description of the actors and carries that description to its logical conclusion—the fanatic terrorist. The article by Dr. Friedman, Fredrica Mann and Dr. Adelman was selected on the basis of its empirical findings and generalizable conclusions. Their thesis is that the gang members are as victimized as society as a whole. That perspective is both intriguing and serves as food for thought. Another insight into the understanding of gang violence is provided by Dr. Man's article, whose thesis is that the violent nature of youth, if not studied further with the goal of eradication, may lead to the very dissolution of society as we know of it today. I endorse Dr. Man's thesis and have found that the violent youth of today will probably become the violent adults of tomorrow. I fear we might have neglected this problem in the past. That neglect is made very explicit by examining the violence in one evening's television programming.

Although I may seem pessimistic, I should not be accused of giving up on society. The people of this country can, when both informed and motivated, take the necessary steps to solve any social problem. I share my experiences and observations with the goal of informing the public. It is then up to that public to become motivated and eradicate our problems.

TYPICAL TERRORISM

One need not be a student of social science to come to realize that a goodly number of our fellow human beings find it difficult to adjust to the will of the majority, or at least the will of the dominant majority and, in fact, have no intention to do so. That negative reaction to the norm may cause the greater social collective some real concerns. It is that small negativistic sub-culture within this whole that needs to be examined. Who are they? What is their motivation for acting out their fears and frustrations on the society as a whole? What can we expect from them in their fright? What are their actions?

As a means of answering those questions, or at least one of them, let us turn to "Who are they?" To the casual newspaper reader, the "boob-tube watcher," or the park bench philosopher, they are little more than "social trash." They serve no real purpose in this life other than to foul things up for the rest of society. On the contrary, though, there may be a more precise term for labeling these outcasts and one that sends shivers up and down our backs. The term that is more popular now than ever before as a label of those negativistic reactionaries is *terrorists!*

The terrorist is usually described by his or her acts, rather than by the individual characteristics he reflects. A definition of some sort is in order to develop a meeting of the minds, so to speak, between the reader and the author. Terrorism is defined as **a tactic or technique by means of which a violent act or the threat thereof is used for the prime purpose of creating overwhelming fear for coercive purposes.***

*National Advisory Committee on Criminal Justice Standards and Goals. *Report of the Task Force on Disorders and Terrorism.* Page 3.

To delineate that all-encompassing definition, it must be understood that terrorism may be constituted or manifested as either an act or threat. There seems to be a growing realization that some of our society's members simply cannot cope! These reactionary groups of people, who seem to display little or no tolerance of the real world concerns, encompass the most visible members of the potential terrorist community today as they have historically. We cite as cause for their behavior mental deficiency, nutritional imbalance, or the ingestion of synthetic substances. We speculate that their maladjustment to society may have been aggravated by abnormal body size, or problems in early childhood, adolescence or with motherhood. The theories go on and on. The fact of the matter is, those individuals are achievers of goals, regardless of the means used for achievement. They are calculators of the risks involved in their struggle. In many cases, they use sophisticated forms of clandestine warfare techniques. They use unique weaponry, and are viciously dangerous. Individual members are uniquely distinguishable, but as a group are very similar in many respects.

As was mentioned, they are unique individually, but the typical terrorist or gang member is a conformist as well. The dynamics of peer pressure, fear of rejection, and the prevalence of various thought disorders in gang members all substantiate this. The terrorist conforms to a small group's norms. They could be called members of social or play groups. They hang around together as often as possible if they're adolescents, and may live and work together if they are adults. In many cases they are like time bombs, terrified of their own potential for loss of control and frightened at what they might do. As they group together this fear seems to dissipate and they find strength in their collectiveness.

Their attitudes fluctuate, both individually and collectively, between guilt and contentment. They employ what social psychologists label "projection dynamics," e.g. "I had a rotten childhood, so I ripped-off some people! Now I'm feeling guilty. But why do I feel guilty? I had the stuff coming." They rationalize and neutralize those acts that are wrong. Inside their heads they wage a war between those "projection dynamics," like the paranoid individual, and their feelings of remorse. Eventually they neutralize those ambivalent or guilt feelings. Simply, they are now thrill-a-moment people by illogical inference. They usually have a skewed thinking pattern, which I call the "wavy fence syndrome." They reason as follows: A is related to B. B is related to C. Therefore, A must be related to C when, in fact, there is no connection. It is at this juncture that they discharge impulses to counter-balance their thought disorder. Their symptomology includes poor control of these impulses and poor identification with primary relationships, which leads to externalizing inappropriate behavior and the rationale for superego-lucanae ("It is cool to be bad" or "They had it coming"). There are no more excuses. There is no turning back or misgivings. They have moved into the sociopathic world.

Eventually, the reasons for their actions are not as important as they once were. Action becomes their most important concern. One can clearly watch this process. The preparation begins. Propaganda assists in the re-thinking of one's original values into a new set of alternative values. The need for control becomes apparent. Members coerce each other just to maintain the cadre. Sometimes drugs are used to stimulate excitement in the membership of the group. The dynamics of justifying the existence of the group begins to circulate like the bubblings of a mineral spring. Enthusiasm is almost at an all-time high. There are no longer any emotional attachments with the rest of society. They are an end unto themselves and their newly assimilated ideals.

As this last stage in their evolution is completed, the newly evolved terrorist group formally exists. It is a mature terrorist organization. The members have buried their former non-utilitarian behavior, malicious mischief or simple acts of vandalism. They have moved from their former feelings of isolation to a feeling of spiritual oneness. The grief and concern of the once-lame ego are now gone. The individual member now feels that before society there now stands a retributive, all-powerful, and artistic super-being who has made a commitment to reaction toward those who would hurt him. He is now a protector that is willing to take any life as well as give his own for what is, in his own lexicon, JUST. Society has been witness and parent to the conception, gestation and birth of the Lone Ranger of the modern era. The Super-Being that discharges wrath on impulse. The *fighter* of the enemy. His immature behavior and anxiety reactions have been channeled into supporting a cause. The individual has worked on preparedness, become organized, become stimulated and well-trained, and now needs a scapegoat. Internal dynamics and the lack of ability to reckon with or dissipate that aggression now leaves the true terrorist with no alternative but to ATTACK.

THE ACTORS

There are as many definitions of who terrorists and gang members are and what they constitute as there are social philosophers or theorists. From my review of the literature and my field observations I view the terrorists and gang members within our society as individuals who do not really differ in any substantive way. The behavior of these individuals involves gestures, actions, situations, and meetings that lead to the provocation and promotion of violence. There are some differences, however. Political terrorists usually move away from ties with their families, often lose any gainful employment they may have had, begin to lose their appetite, sexual desires, and gradually show their only signs of ego-assertion in situations where they are interacting with fellow terrorists. Members of street gangs and outlaw motorcycle gangs normally do not have a preconceived notion about the political and social conditions of the world, whereas political terrorists may find motivation from those existing social conditions.

Collectively, both political terrorists and gang members seldom show each other genuine warmth and human interaction. Rather, their communication and interaction is typified by coercing one another. They often use sexual erotica coupled with violence or degradation as a stimulus for an emotional and spiritual re-thinking of the outside world.

Gangs many times develop from cohesive "play groups" or "secondary social groups." They become a neighborhood cadre or school social group and slowly evolve into violent actors. Whether their behavior is delinquent acted-out or adult acted-out, it is nearly always characterized by harm and violence to others. Probably one of the most unique characteristics of that violence revolves around its victim. Victims seldom have any relationship that is directly related to the group or its targets. Victims are simply, "in the wrong place at the wrong time," unless, of course, the victim is a rival of some sort.

Too often this predilection towards violence is more easily managed by the power structure by simply not telling society the facts. If that be the case, I will tell you now, those groups have a predisposition towards violence! They are not going to be any less violent because the public is ignorant of their actions nor will public awareness diminish the group's ability for and motivation to violence. Their bizarre sociopathic behavior must be reckoned with and society must be aware of their tactics and predispositions in order to lessen its vulnerability.

The classic terrorist actor also exhibits other traits that the reader might want to become familiar with in order to develop a greater understanding of these individuals. These "kinky" individuals who actively enjoy violence and sadism make no attempt to lessen or denature their pervasive urge to be violent. They approach violence in a sort of ceremonial way by reading about it, talking about it, practicing gestures, making weapons, et cetera. They champion sadism by blending in just enough altruism to keep them from self-damage and self-destruction.

Terrorists tend to adhere to some supernatural notion of "power control" beyond them, while periodically bolting out at society with behavior that attacks society's moral, spiritual and political structure. Many terrorists are victims of their own victimization, as the articles by Drs. Friedman and Man relate. They are like small children who are seized in a park while picnicking. The attacker kidnaps them, assaults them, and holds them captive while repeatedly ridiculing and re-assaulting them. Then, all of a sudden, the child as victim becomes enthralled with his captor and may soon become inspired and eventually intellectually reborn as attacker himself. The sodomizing of new prison gang members, as Mark's case in the first part of this book illustrates, is the first step to acceptance of the group's identity and power in exchange for the initiate's old identity. Recent articles and radio and television broadcasts further this illustration. The statements by members of contemporary gangs now facing criminal prosecution, and by some of those that have been sentenced to prison, all seem to support this member-as-victim phenomena.

Nearly every member of a violent organization is in a mind-battle between self-preservation and antagonism. The old cliche, "guilt by association," certainly fits in well here. The antisocial behavior of an individual member can be reinforced until the desire to break away from the group no longer exists. The confused zealot has come to the end of his acting career in this morbid fantasy. He has literally become a permanent member of an organization for the remainder of his puzzled and confused life. With few exceptions, he may have willingly become a victim of his own victimization. At that point, he had internalized the group's identity and may progress into the theater of the fanatic.

To better familiarize the reader with a social definition of fanaticism, which may serve to identify the actors as well as the process discussed in this writing, I have chosen to include the following article, "The Social Meaning of Fanaticism," prepared by Professor Stanley Milgram of the City University of New York's Graduate Center. It should serve to inform the reader of the nature of the fanatic as he relates to our study of gangs and terrorism.

THE SOCIAL MEANING OF FANATICISM*

by

Stanley Milgram

The term *Fanaticism* appeared in the English language in the seventeenth century, and in its initial usage referred to *excessive enthusiasm* in religious belief. In modern times its usage has been extended to include unreasonable enthusiasm in political, as well as cultural pre-occupations; but except in its truncated form, *fan* (such as a Beatle *fan*), it has never lost its pejorative sense.

A fanatic is someone who goes to extremes in beliefs, feelings, and actions. In principle, extremity of feeling need not be negatively evaluated, but may be signified with such positive terms as *passionate involvement, undaunted commitment,* and *profound religiosity.* The term *fanaticism,* therefore, is applied to the state of mind of those who are wholeheartedly committed to a set of beliefs and are condemned for it.

But why should the enthusiasm which envelops the fanatic's beliefs be condemned? First, because such enthusiasm is excessive to the point of creating an intellectual deficit. The high pitch of emotion enveloping fanatical belief is more than a substitute for thought, it is a barrier: the fanatic is closed to argument and reason. Intellectual rigidity undergirds his thought. The fanatic lacks critical judgment and is blind to the contradictions of his own position. (Thus youthful religious fanatics exalt a doctrine of *love,* but fail to extend the feeling to the families they callously abandon.) They say about fanatics that "you can't talk to them." Insofar as the purpose of talk is an exchange of ideas and possible mutual persuasion, the fanatic is not a viable conversationalist.

*Reprinted from *Et cetera,* Vol. XXXIV, No. 1 by permission of the International Society for General Semantics.

We often share the ends or values of the fanatic, but decry the single-mindedness with which he pursues them, and his failure to accommodate to the normal requirements of social life. His purity and unstinting commitment to these values is perceived as unreasonable, excessive, and injurious to the complex fabric of social life. For his beliefs come to assume an extraordinarily central role in his life, with an accompanying devaluation of all other values and relationships. In the face of fanatical belief, life-long allegiances to family and kin may be abandoned. (Thus the pathetic sight of families picketing a rally of the Reverend Sun Myung Moon, who has induced their progeny to a state of fanatical devotion.)

Some degree of mutual accommodation among individuals is a precondition of a viable society. Each individual must, in some degree, attempt to see the needs of the other, unless life is to be characterized by constant friction and conflict. But the purity of the fanatic's conviction does not make this possible. The fanatic is a threat because the intensity and obduracy of his belief remove him from the normal possibility of influence and mutual accommodation which are in the long run necessary conditions for the maintenance of social order.

If the fanatic's beliefs are impervious to change, yet a pressure toward homogeneity of belief is exerted when people live in society, logic dictates that society itself may have to undergo an accommodative transformation. Thus, in the long run, fanaticism may serve as a mechanism of social change. Indeed, history offers notable examples of groups whose fanatical beliefs were initially scorned, but which ultimately prevailed through the conversion of an entire society to their point of view.

One of the most striking features of fanaticism is the discrepancy between the inner experience and the outer appearance. Although the fanatic may be aware that others decry his behavior, he sees himself acting out of noble motives. Indeed, a striking symmetry operates in the perception of the fanatic by others, and his own perception of the majority. The majority thinks that the fanatic's deviant beliefs and behavior constitute a problem, but unlike the penitent, or the criminal who knows he is committing crimes, the fanatic sees the problem residing in the majority. It is they who do not see the point that animates all his actions. In the fanatic's eyes, the others have not grasped the truth and thus are behaving strangely, and even destructively.

Every episode of fanaticism has a natural history. Frequently, there is a point of conversion when the potential fanatic "sees the light," leading to a sudden shift in his demeanor and beliefs. The fanatical impulse has expression not only in beliefs but in behavior which clashes with that of the immediate surroundings. This frequently evokes criticism, and efforts on the part of those close to the fanatic to persuade him to abandon his deviant ways. The fanatical impulse may rigidify and remain a permanent feature of the individual's personality, or it may run its course, wither in the absence of social support. On the other hand, a group of likeminded fanatics may band together to form a community within which the deviant beliefs are mutually reinforced and legitimized.

The street on which I work is now frequented by devoted adherents to the Reverend Sun Myung Moon, a Korean industrialist, the leader of a variant Christian sect. Members of the sect accost passersby, hand out leaflets, and attempt to proselytize for the Reverend Moon's cause. The characteristic reaction of the public is one of derision or scorn. Many have commented that the glazed eyes, steadfastness of aim, and inappropriateness of behavior mark the "Moonies" as religious fanatics. To be sure, that phase of the relationship between the deviant group and the larger society in which the group is termed *fanatical* precedes by several stages the capitulation of society to the fanatic's beliefs. Perhaps in the next century society will speak of these adherents with the reverence now accorded to the disiciples of Christ.

But capitulation is by no means the only possible outcome. The fanatical belief may spontaneously fade; the fanatics may be isolated within the society (through ghettos or internal exile); they may be forced to emigrate; or they may be destroyed.

Fanaticism is in many ways the opposite of "keeping cool," and thus is opposed to the hip culture which recently dominated the most advanced segments of our youth. Perhaps there is an inevitable alternation in these two attitudes; and, if that is so, we may expect an imminent increase in the variety and intensity of fanatical groups.

For a social scientist, fanaticism raises a number of interesting empirical issues. The first is a question in personality research: Are some individuals more likely than others to become fanatics? And if so, what are the personality characteristics of such individuals and the antecedent conditions of such development? There are a number of investigations, such as that of Professor Milton Rokeach on the open and closed mind, that point to certain specific cognitive styles that predispose a person to fanatical adherence to doctrine.

Second: Is fanaticism merely a matter of degree, a slight intensification of feeling, or is there a significant qualitative shift to a new state of mental organization? Many look at the Moonies as if something fundamental had snapped, some balance wheel been thrown out of kilter. My own hypothesis is that for the fanatic, the belief system comes to be central to his identity, the kingpin of an ego-defensive system, so that any criticism of the belief automatically implies a threat to his self esteem. Fanatical belief often serves as a therapeutic crutch to persons desperately staving off a collapse of self worth.

Third: What sociological conditions are likely to give rise to fanatical groups, and as a corollary question, what structural conditions of society are conducive to labeling others as fanatics? Could it be that the greater the degree of homogeneity and conformity in a society, the more readily are deviant beliefs labelled as fanaticism?

Fanaticism serves not only as a descriptive term, but as an explanatory category. Thus the desecration of a reform temple is thought to be "explained" by asserting that it was the work of religious fanatics.

Yet the term, insofar as it constitutes a pejorative label applied by the majority to a deviant minority, possesses an intractable ambiguity. How do we distinguish between fanaticism and the commendable adherence to principle? Is the Pope fanatical in his adherence to outdated notions of birth control? Are the Amish fanatics because they live by an older culture and resist the influence of the modern world? There is no answer to this question other than in the pragmatics of the term. The word, like most depreciatory labels, has its uses.

Indeed, it may be applied prematurely to those who possess a truth which others have not yet perceived. The label may thus serve a defensive function, in denying legitimacy to the claims of those whose beliefs and principles differ from our own.

JUVENILE STREET GANGS: THE VICTIMIZATION OF YOUTH

C. Jack Friedman, Ph.D., Fredrica Mann and Howard Adelman, Ph.D.

INTRODUCTION

Although there have been many reports on street gangs, there are none which focus on the victimization of members. In Philadelphia, where gangs have been blamed for about forty homicides a year, and about tenfold more serious injuries to gang members and innocent bystanders, there has been insufficient research concerning the victimization of gang members by their peers. This research was intended to elucidate the nature and extent of victimization of gang affiliated youths in comparison with non-gang control subjects. Street gang members were compared with a matched group of non-members from the same neighbor-

ADOLESCENCE, Vol. XI No. 44, Winter 1976. Libra Publishers, Inc.

hoods on self-reports of illegal and, sometimes dangerous, acts which they were forced to commit by gang members.

METHOD

Subjects

Subjects were 486 adolescent males out of a total sample of 536 who completed a questionnaire which included selected items characterizing the victimization of youths by the gang. These youths were between 15 and 18 years of age; 61% were black, and 39% were white. The sources of subjects were as follows: 198 were selected from three residential, correctional institutions; 160 were selected from a community-based job-training program for the "hard-core" unemployed; and 128 were recruited from a local, inner-city public high school. Sampling of youths from the correctional institutions and from the community-based job-training program was by consecutive admissions. Sampling of the public high school students was by intact advisory classes; and students were assigned alphabetically, thereby avoiding bias in curriculum and level of skill. Of five such advisory classes sampled, 80% or more of all eligible males volunteered to participate. Thus, the sampling procedures reduced volunteer bias. All subjects were from the lower social strata of Philadelphia and vicinity according to the Hollingshead-Redlich socio-economic status classifications.

Of the 486 subjects, 270 admitted belonging to a gang. The reliability of the self-report information about the affiliations of subjects, including names and locations, was checked with the gang control unit of the Philadelphia Police Department. For all but three black subjects, it was possible to verify the existence, name, and location of the gang to which they belonged. Police verification of information on white gangs was not complete. Previous analyses comparing white and black street gang members revealed three basic differences which would explain the difficulty for law enforcement authorities to identify white gangs. First, white gang members were not territorially bound. They more often identified their gang by a location than by a name. Finally, they less often characterized the gang as having a structure and leadership hierarchy.

Victimization Questionnaire

Information on subjects was obtained from a self-report questionnaire. One group of times comprising the questionnaire characterized forced illegal activities. The 22 victimization items were developed from discussions with known gang members and with gang workers; from information contained in a report from the Governor's Justice Commission on Gang Violence; and from family therapists who worked extensively with this kind of population.

The questionnaire was administered in booklet form and subjects were directed to follow along with an audio tape narration of the material. This procedure of using an audio tape was intended to aid subjects with weak reading skills. Subjects responded by checking items which were identified by number on the taped narrative. Prior experience with this procedure suggested that subjects were less inhibited responding to an audio-tape than a face-to-face interview with a psychological examiner where lack of anonymity could be a problem.

For these 22 victimization items, subjects were asked, "Whether or not you are or ever have been a member of a gang, have you been made to do any of the following things by members of a gang." Subjects were directed to check as many of the following acts as they were forced to commit:

Analyses of Data

Percentages were computed for groups of gang affiliates and non-affiliates for the 22 items. Comparisons were made between gang affiliates and non-affiliates by Chi Square Analyses. These results are presented in Table 1.

TABLE 1

COMPARISONS BETWEEN STREET GANG MEMBERS AND NON-MEMBERS AS TO ANTISOCIAL AND ILLEGAL ACTS WITH WHICH THEY WERE FORCED TO COMMIT BY GANGS

Item	% Gang	% Non-Gang	Chi Square
Stay out all night long	17	16	.3
Cause trouble in the neighborhood	21	13	4.5*
Call policemen names	22	14	5.2*
Get drunk	32	16	16.9**
Bother grownups in your own neighborhood or another neighborhood	15	10	3.3
Fight	44	21	28.9**
Get a weapon or hide a weapon	22	12	21.2**
Stab someone or injure someone with a weapon	22	10	11.9**
Shoot at someone	25	9	20.7**
Take heroin, "scag" or "smack"	7	8	0
Have sex with a girl	38	14	33.4**
Have sex with other guys	4	3	.5
Steal	27	13	13.8**
Fight at school	38	18	22.9**
Skip homework	25	9	20.0**
Take pot, grass, reefers, hash or marihuana	20	15	2.0
Stay away from school	24	13	4.9*
"Shake down" other guys	24	33	4.9*
Take speed or meth or methadrine	7	6	0
Break up parties	26	9	24.6**
Destroy public property	20	12	6.1**
Mark or spray paint on walls	30	15	15.7**

*p .05
**p .01

For the group of gang members, further comparisons were made between black and white youths on the 22 items by Chi Square Analyses. These results are shown in Table 2.

RESULTS

Table 1, which shows the results of the comparison of street gang members and non-members, reveals that significantly more gang affiliates reported that they were forced to "cause trouble in the neighborhood," "call policemen names," "get drunk," "fight," "get or hide a weapon," "stab or injure someone with a weapon," "shoot at someone with a gun," "steal," "fight at school," "skip homework," "stay away from school," "break up parties," "destroy public property," and "mark or spray paint walls." There was only one reversal of this trend. Significantly more non-members reported that they had been forced to "shake down" other guys. There were no significant differences between street gang members and non-members on the three drug abuse items, or on being forced to "stay out all night long," or "bother grown-ups."

TABLE 2

COMPARISONS BETWEEN BLACK STREET GANG MEMBERS AND WHITE STREET GANG MEMBERS AS TO ANTISOCIAL & ILLEGAL ACTS WHICH THEY WERE FORCED TO COMMIT BY GANGS

Item	% Affirmative Responses White Street Gang	Black Street Gang	Chi Square
Stay out all night long	26	13	6.9**
Cause trouble in the neighborhood	26	18	2.3
Call policemen names	27	19	2.2
Get drunk	33	31	0
Bother grownups in your own neighborhood or another neighborhood	22	12	4.2*
Fight	39	47	1.8
Get a weapon or hide a weapon	25	31	1.1
Stab someone or injure someone with a weapon	15	25	3.5
Shoot at someone	18	28	3.4
Take heroin, "scag" or "smack"	10	66	1.1
Have sex with a girl	35	39	0
Have sex with other guys	6	4	0
Steal	27	26	0
Fight at school	33	40	1.3
Skip homework	27	21	1.4
Take pot, grass, reefers, hash or marihuana	46	16	29.0**
Stay away from school	27	23	0
"Shake down" other guys	18	27	2.5
Take speed or meth or methadrine	8	67	0.2
Break up parties	26	26	0
Destroy public property	23	19	0.4
Mark or spray paint on walls	24	33	2.3

*p .05

**p .01

A substantial proportion of non-members who lived in neighborhoods where there were street gangs, reported being forced to commit a variety of delinquent acts. 33% reported being forced by street gangs to "shake down other guys"; 21% were forced to "fight"; 18% reported being forced to "fight at school"; 16% reported being forced to "get drunk"; 16% to "stay out all night long"; about 15% were forced to "take pot, grass, reefers, hash or marijuana"; 15% to "mark or spray paint walls"; and between 15% and 14% were forced to "call policemen names," "have sex with a girl," "have sex with other guys," "cause trouble in the neighborhood," "stay away from school," "steal," "get or hide a weapon," and "destroy public property." It is especially noteworthy that 10% of the non-members were made to "stab someone or injure someone with a weapon," 9% were forced to "shoot at someone with a gun," and 8% were forced to "take heroin, scag or smack." The reader should keep in mind that these responses only indicate the number of subjects who reported being forced to engage in the behaviors presented and not the number of times that each individual engaged in that behavior.

There were three significant differences between black and white street gang members as to activities which they were forced to commit by the gang. Significantly more white street gang members reported being coerced by the gang to "stay out all night long," "bother grown-ups in your own neighborhood or another neighborhood," and "take pot, grass, reefers, hash or marijuana."

CONCLUSIONS AND DISCUSSIONS

This study was an empirical survey of the victimization of gang affiliates and non-affiliates of street gangs in Philadelphia. The most important finding emanating from this research was the nature and extent of violent behavior instigated and committed by street gang members. For example, 25% of the subjects in this study who identified themselves as members of street gangs and 9% of the subjects who denied any street gang affiliation reported that they had been forced *to shoot at someone with a gun.* This coercive and violent aspect of street gang behavior poses the most critical challenge to those who advocate and are charged with developing programs to defuse, dismantle, or redirect the antisocial and criminal activities of street gangs. If these patterns of behavior continue to be associated with the functions of the street gang over a long enough period of time, they are likely to become autonomous, expected, and highly resistant to change. It is therefore important to elucidate the nature of the influence of the street gang on members and non-members alike as well as determine the mechanisms by which the street gang gains power over the individual. The present study is a step in this direction.

For the most part, race did not play a significant role in this study. The few differences between black and white subjects indicated more rebellion towards adults and use of drugs by white gang and non-gang members alike.

The main findings from this study indicate that street gangs in Philadelphia appear to be different in certain essential ways from the gangs in other cities. In Philadelphia, the rituals of street gang warfare and the practices of victimizing both gang members and non-members by forcing them to commit serious and violent offenses may serve to maintain the continuity of the group, to give it structure, and to symbolize the gang's power of life and death over others. There is evidence from the present findings of an orderly progression of direct challenges by the gang to the established authority of the family, the community, the school, the police, and finally to the individual himself. For example, the street gang thwarts the authority of the family by making its members and others stay out all night long and challenges the authority of persons in the community by spray painting walls and bothering or intimidating grown-ups in the neighborhood. Street gang members prevent high school students from attending school by establishing gang "turfs" which can be crossed only at the risk of a physical confrontation and by initiating fights in the schools. Encouragement of the use of drugs and alcohol perhaps serves the dual purpose of providing an exciting activity and alienating street gang members from adults in the community. Although the police may represent a powerful counterforce to the street gang, gang members can be made to call policemen names and to resist arrest. Acts of property destruction, which yield no material gains and which would not seem to gratify the excitement needs of those who commit such offenses, probably have as their purpose the further separation of each gang member from the values of the larger community. Gang members, who become further separated and alienated from family, community, and law enforcement institutions may eventually have no choice but to become more dependent upon and allied with the gang. The ultimate demonstration of the influence of the street gang over its members and non-members is the capacity to make an individual commit a life threatening act—to shoot a gun at someone or to put himself forward as the target of a rival gang.

The authority with which the street gang influences its members represents nearly absolute control of the group over the behavior of the individual. It probably takes relatively few exemplary incidents to convince all of the members that they must either submit to the gang's decisions or face more personally destructive consequences.

It is not clear whether this hypothesized process by which the individual who joins a gang is selectively separated and alienated from the family, school, and mainstream society is conscious or planned. Many gang-affiliated youths have no family or other social resources to support them. Their families were fragmented and disorganized; the schools were unable to contain them or provide them with sufficient educational skills to compete and adjust in our complex society; and the larger, middle-class community offered limited opportunities and even less hope for future, productive employment. Many of the boys who joined a street gang may also have been coerced into doing so to avoid having to live with the ever-present threat of retaliation by gang members in their neighborhoods. These pressures may have been even more intense for black youth, for whom the neighborhoods are cordoned into "turfs" with defined boundaries. It may, therefore, have been that boys who later joined street gangs were prone to do so because they were deprived by family and society rather than because they consciously rejected the authority of the family, schools, police, and community. However, those individuals in this study who did not join street gangs lived in these same neighborhoods, went to the same inner-city public high schools or work programs, came from comparably structured families with the same economic limitations and were subjected to the same kinds of pressures. A more detailed discussion of differences found in this subject sample between gang members and non-members from the same neighborhoods is presented in an article entitled, "A Profile of Juvenile Street Gang Members."

AGGRESSIVE BEHAVIOR AND VIOLENCE OF YOUTH: APPROACHES AND ALTERNATIVES

by

Man Keung Ho, Ph.D. *

Associate Professor, School of Social Work, University of Oklahoma

Aggressive behavior and violence constitute the single most prevalent cause for youth's direct contact with correctional workers and law enforcement agencies. It is imperative, therefore, that correctional workers understand the origin of aggression and violence before attempting to help young persons cope with their violent and aggressive behavior.

*Reprinted from *Federal Probation Quarterly,* Vol. XXXIX. March 1975, No. 1.

This article describes the nature and differences between aggression and violence; emotional hazards of correctional workers in dealing with aggressive and violent youth; the correctional worker's use of self, techniques, and skills; and limits in working with this group.

Nature and Difference Between Aggression and Violence

Violence generally results from a spirit that is out of harmony with its situation, subjective or objective. Much of this disturbance of the spirit may never manifest itself in visible physical ways. Too often correctional workers have attempted to treat the surface manifestations of a youth's aggression and have neglected the inner turbulence that produced the overt acts. Aggression, as described in *Control of Aggression and Violence,* edited by Jerome Singer,[1] may be: (1) active or passive, (2) direct or indirect, (3) physical or verbal with various combinations in various situations. Despite the limited success of the bio-behavioral approach to understanding human violence that has recently been reported,[2] there is no consensus as to the source and purpose of aggression. However, there is enough evidence to indicate that aggressiveness is instinctive, and that it has certain useful and constructive functions. The innate drives that manifest themselves as assertiveness, aggressiveness and violence may be essential to the survival of humanity in a competitive situation. While Konrad Lorenz[3] thought that both the instigations to and the inhibitions of aggressiveness were innate, Sigmund Freud[4] believed that the inhibitions were socially acquired and learned during childhood. Such

1. Jerome Singer. *The Control of Aggression and Violence.* New York: Academic Press, 1971.

2. Frank Ochberg, "Theories of Violence," paper presented at the Fifth Annual Seminar sponsored by Children's Medical Center, Tulsa, Oklahoma, October 1973. Bio-behavioral approach refers to the understanding of behavior through the biological makeup of a person.

3. Konrad Lorenz, *On Aggression.* New York: Harcourt, Brace & World, 1966.

4. Sigmund Freud, *Group Psychology and the Analysis of the Ego.* London: The Hogarth Press, 1948.

implications indicate why the concept of the origin of aggressions is so important. If it is merely an inevitable factor of human nature, correctional workers are wasting time trying to rid themselves of it. If, on the other hand, the instigations to aggression and/or the restraints or inhibitions of aggression are socially acquired and subject to being conditioned by training, education, or alteration of environment, there is much that correctional workers can do to help the aggressive and violent youth. It is here that the social learning school of thought makes its contribution and also serves as a springboard to the following discussions related to the approaches and alternatives for channeling aggression and violence into socially acceptable behavior.

Before approaches and alternatives to aggression and violence can be discussed meaningfully, a clear definition of each is necessary. Aggression is that behavior largely inborn but modulated through learning, which is intrusive, assertive, and concerned with dominance and advancement. It is used in contradistinction to passivity and docility, and it is certainly not "bad."

Violence, on the other hand, is needlessly destructive. By definition, violence is "bad" whether or not it is intentional, rational, or criminal. It is that which is needlessly destructive of life, and brings physical pain, emotional anguish, or societal disruption. Implicit in the above definition is that of the role of a correctional worker which is to help youth realize accept, and channel aggression into socially accepted behavior and goals, and simultaneously to help youth comprehend and surmount their violent tendencies.

Worker Awareness and Attitudes

Violent youth usually are extremely resistant to treatment of any sort involving external assistance. For a correctional worker to successfully treat violent youth he must additionally be aware of emotional hazards, such as the use of rejection and denial, involved in the treatment process. Furthermore, a violent youth tends to boast about his hostile, violent act. This usually intensifies the worker's fear of violence, feeling of uncontrol, rage, and anger at the youth whom he is to help. By so doing, the worker also is dealing with his own anger at the youth by projecting the anger onto him and thus perceiving him as being more dangerous than he really is. Accordingly, the worker may then become more fearful, but in reality he is fearful of his own anger.

The aggressive behavior and violence displayed by a youth can easily influence a worker to adopt a more repressive approach that could entail the youth or physically seclude him. His abandonment of the youth as a means to handle his fear and anger of him can easily be sensed by the youth himself who usually responds with a greater degree of anxiety. Thus, withdrawal is a common emotional hazard of correctional workers in dealing with violent youth. The correctional worker who neglects a violent youth and uses denial as a means of dealing with his dangerousness is ubiquitous. Unfortunately, the youth will sense fully the worker's rejection and will respond by becoming more anxious and aggressive.

A correctional worker should recognize his authority relationship,[5] along with the emotional hazards he generally experiences. Should he be preoccupied with his status as a professional, and as an authority figure representing a law enforcement or related agency, he tends to be threatened easily by the youth's aggressive behavior which merely is a manifestation of his loneliness or fear of being nobody. Conversely, should a correctional worker have failed to resolve successfully his own conflicts with an authority figure(s) in the past, he will tend to encourage the youth to aggressively act out resentment and violence toward authority for the vicarious experience. This encounter will only reinforce and intensify the worker's violence and anxiety.

Ideally, a correctional worker should be able to enter an interdependent working relationship with a youth. Only through an interdependent relationship, can the youngster securely experience giving and receiving in a problem-solving

5. This refers to three kinds of authority relationships: dependence, independence, and interdependence.

situation with a worker who neither condones nor is threatened by his aggressive behavior.

Techniques and Skills

Application of catharsis principle. — Once a correctional worker is secure with his own authority relationship position, his encounter with an aggressive youngster may be guided by the catharsis principle. This principle refers to the liberation of affect through the reexperiencing of blocked or inhibited emotions, which is supposedly an essential phase in the resolution of unconscious conflicts.[6] In applying the principle to aggressive behavior, the occurrence of any act of aggression is assumed to reduce the instigation to aggression.[7] Bettelheim,[8] therefore, recommends that children be allowed to experience violence under controlled conditions to avoid bottling up aggressive potential that could erupt later in an explosive outbreak. Correctional workers whose treatment techniques have almost exclusively relied on verbal interaction must recognize other potentially valuable methods. Innovative techniques based on specific adolescent needs should be explored. The author's experience in adopting the "Chinese Fire Drill" as a catharsis technique in working with a group of hard-core delinquents is an example where controlled violence was essential for the aggressive young persons to gradually work through their unconscious conflicts and learned violence of the past.[9]

From playing out to talking out. — Despite the increasing tendency for the worker to engage the aggressive youth in the controlled acting out or playing out activities, there is

6. S. Feshback, "The Catharsis, Hypothesis and Some Consequences of Interaction With Aggressive and Neutral Play Objects," *Journal of Personality,* May 1956.

7. J. Dollard, et al., *Frustration and Aggression.* New Haven: Yale University Press, 1939, p. 50.

8. B. Bettelheim, "Children Should Learn About Violence," *Saturday Evening Post,* 240, March 1967.

9. M. Ho, "The Use of Contract in Group Therapy with Hard-Core Delinquents," paper originally presented at the 1973 American Group Psychotherapy Association Annual Conference at Detroit, Michigan, February 1973. "Chinese Fire Drill" is a game which allows players to run about, screaming and yelling.

also a need for him to encourage the latter to learn how to express *verbally* his aggression and potential violence. The worker's ability to empathize with the youngster is indispensable, because expression of feeling, especially negative feeling for the first time, necessitates a nonthreatening and trusting relationship and climate created by the worker's non-judgmental attitude and sincere concern. Since the expression of feelings necessitates one's ability to first label them, the worker's role in working with a violent youngster is more than that of a facilitator; it is also that of a teacher.

When Johnny was describing the incident in which he was physically assaulted by his father, the worker asked how he felt at that particular moment. Johnny replied, "I tried to pick up whatever I could find to hit him back." "This was what you did, but you have yet to tell me how you actually felt," remarked the worker. After a few minutes of struggle (with the help of the worker), Johnny was able to express that he was extremely fearful, angry, and "pissed off" at his father at that time. As Johnny learned to label his feelings and express them, he began to improve. He discovered that hitting back physically was not the only means of responding to a situation.

The discussion then shifted toward helping Johnny examine the difficulty he experienced at school when he constantly attempted to resolve conflicts by physical violence with authority figures. As the treatment continued, Johnny was able to express his resentment verbally toward the teachers without resorting to physical attacks which had kept him expelled from the school during most of the school term.

The technique of "doubling."—Despite the growing need for an aggressive youngster to express verbally instead of physically, a youngster from an emotionally deprived and physically violent home environment usually is not taught to verbally express himself.[10] In helping a younger youth to

10. See Robert Sears and Harry Levin, "The Sources of Aggression in the Home," in *Patterns of Child Rearing.* New York: Harper & Row, 1957, pp. 255-263; and Jules Henry, "Making Pete Tough," in *Culture Against Man.* Random House, 1963.

express his inner feelings, the technique of "doubling" is especially applicable.

Robert, age 12, came from a large family where his parents rarely had the opportunity to talk with him alone. His repeated outbursts of temper at school resulted in considerable property damage and ultimately his suspension from school. In the second interview, the worker sensed the repeated frustration which Robert had experienced in verbally expressing his feelings, despite his apparent willingness to do so. The worker then placed a solid chair and a sandbag in front of Robert and instructed him to use them whenever he desired. Once Robert had expressed himself through physically handling the chair or sandbag, the worker would attempt to explain verbally how Robert felt at that particular moment. If the worker's explanation was inaccurate, Robert was encouraged to help the worker correct it. Correcting Robert's behavior required many attempts by the worker, but the learning experience eventually allowed Robert to express himself verbally rather than physically. The following example illustrates this point:

After the worker had explained to Robert the incidence that took place in the classroom, he played the role of the classmate who antagonized Robert by calling him "shortie." (Worker knew previously that Robert was very sensitive to others calling him shortie.) Robert apparently was not annoyed at the first few name callings, but gradually lost humor when the worker continued persistently. Robert doubled up his fist, but realizing he could not hit the worker, he turned the chair upside down and kicked the sandbag repeatedly. After this had taken place a couple of times, the worker remarked, "I (Robert) am angry, disgusted at you (worker), lay off me!" Robert nodded first, then said that was exactly how he felt. The discussion then focused on the necessity of conveying one's feelings to others without taking physical action, including damaging the classroom furniture.

The technique of doubling also can be applied in working with verbally aggressive youth who tend to intellectualize with words void of any real feeling and action.

Becky, an apparently gregarious youngster, complained frequently of being deprived of affection by her foster parents, especially the foster father. During one interview, the worker was to "double" her feeling. When he moved toward the chair which represented her foster father, Becky was instructed to express the level of affection displayed by the worker. For example, when the worker reached his hands toward the chair, Becky would comment, "I wish to be close to you." When the worker touched the chair, Becky would say, "I would like you to touch me back, or cuddle me." Becky became comfortable in making different affectionate remarks only when the worker approached from the back of the chair (adoptive father), but not from in front of the chair. Subsequent discussions indicated that Becky was sexually threatened by her foster father with whom she was secretly in love but felt extremely guilty about it. She had resorted to resolve her ambivalence through complaints and verbal attacks in order to keep him at a distance.

Integration. — Aggressive behavior and violence can be transformed into verbal attacks and abuses. The real meaning or reasons for aggressive behavior of this form sometimes can be incomprehensible even to the attacker himself who may not actually wish to hurt others. It is essential that a correctional worker encourage the verbally aggressive youngster to examine the congruence and consistency between his words and his real feelings. The following example illustrates this approach and technique.

Susan was a personable, affectionate, but insensitive, girl who always got into trouble with her stepmother, who, although basically very fond of Susan, could not get along well enough with her for them to be in the same house. After helping Susan clarify her ambivalence toward her stepmother, the worker instructed Susan to stand close to the door with her back behind it. The worker, who played the role of her stepmother, chose the opposite door and did likewise. Susan was further instructed to move one step forward should she decide to express verbally something positive to her stepmother. Should Susan choose to express something negative, she was instructed to move one step backward before she did so. The worker followed the same instructions. As Susan was expressing positive thoughts and comments, she found herself reluctantly moving forward and whenever she became conscious of her true feeling and action, she chose to step backward and expressed something negative, which she later regretted claiming she never meant being that hostile toward her stepmother. When she was approached warmly by the stepmother, she immediately withdrew, stepped back, and regretted later. Susan volunteered later during the interview that she really was fond of her stepmother, but feared being rejected by her as she had been by her real mother. Because of her fear, Susan resorted to verbal violence in order to maintain a distance between her and her stepmother.

The treatment exercise employed by the worker vividly demonstrated to Susan the discrepancy between her words and her true feelings, and the part she played in isolating herself from others, especially her stepmother. Such treatment techniques can provide young aggressors a concrete, relevant picture of their problems and also alternatives to problems. It actively involves the youngster in gaining insight which is personally relevant with no unnecessary interpretation and judgment from the worker.

Utilization of drawing. — Since aggression and violence can be expressed passively and indirectly, a correctional worker should not be manipulated into believing that a quiet and "yes sir-no sir" type overtly well-mannered young person is problem-free. Instead, he should realize that the potential aggression and violence on the part of this youngster sometimes is twice as difficult to work with than an overtly aggressive youngster. Should a correctional worker encounter a passively aggressive youngster, his reliance on the traditional verbal-exchange approach usually will result in an impasse and produce further withdrawal by the youngster.

A technique relying on simple drawings on the part of the youngster provides perhaps the only breakthrough in working with some passively aggressive youth. According to Burns and Kaufman, "a youngster's latent aggression and violence can be detected by the manner in which he shades and scribbles his drawings."[11] An aggressive youngster also tends to exert excessive pressure in drawing. Whether his aggression and violence are directed toward others or himself also can be detected by the manner in which he draws. he use of drawing is a viable tool for providing the youngster with an opportunity to express himself, other than talking, which most of them, often with an omnipresent anxiety, are poorly prepared to do.

Whenever a youngster is provided the opportunity to draw and to explain his own drawings freely, he ceases to be cast in a dependent and powerless role. Accordingly, he no longer needs to harbor the aggression he recently needed for the reassurance of his own worth and power. The act of drawing also provides the aggressive youngster with the catharsis and desensitization effects which are essential in overcoming his anxiety associated with aggression.

Utilization of limits. — Violence is destructive aggression resulting from mislearning. The use of limits by a correctional worker to help a violent youngster develop control within himself, therefore, can prove highly valuable. The therapeutic use of limits by the correctional worker can protect the violent youngster from his impulses and provide him with some relief from his overwhelming anxieties. The youngster can also learn that his impulses can be handled without being harmful to himself or others. Further, he feels secure realizing that he cannot and will not damage himself or others. Armed with this new sense of security, the violent youngster also develops a feeling of success which he desperately needs but has never previously experienced.

Obviously, for an impulse-ridden youngster, the acceptance of limits from an authority figure (worker) is never easy. Should the worker enforce limits on a youngster prior to the development of a positive working relationship, the young person will tend to perceive the limits as an intentional threat to castigate him as a nonbeing. Thus, he will respond

11. For detailed information of drawings, see Robert Burns and Harvard Kaufman, *Kinetic Family Drawings.* New York: Brunner/ Mazel 1972.

with greater violence just to reassure his omnipresence. It therefore is no accident that a violent youngster travels from the school principal's office to the state correctional institution, always harboring the attitude that "nobody is going to push me around, including you."

Conversely, a correctional worker who is secure and knowledgeable of his authority relationship, may exert positive influences on the violent youngster whose basic needs, after all, are no different than his. Like all human beings, the violent youngster feels, only more deeply, what Alan Platon expressed: "To mean something in the world is the deepest hunger of the human soul, deeper than any bodily hunger and thirst, and when a man has lost it, he is no longer a man."[12] The essentials required of a correctional worker to establish a positive working relationship with a violent youngster prior to administration of limits include such qualities as clarity of mutual goals and behavioral reinforcement principles including immediacy, relevancy, and consistency. Most important is the worker's attitude toward the youngster as a worthy human being. If the worker's attitude is understanding, accepting, respectful, genuine and trustful, he will become the live human model who is most needed by an emotionally starved youngster who resorts to violence to compensate for his lack of human affection.

Conclusion

Since destructive aggression of a youth is the major concern of the correctional worker, the worker must be aware of his own cultural background and authority relationship position in order to work successfully with violent youngsters. Furthermore, the worker needs to be cognizant of the potential emotional hazards inherent in working with rebellious violent youth. Despite the growing need for encouraging resistive, anxiety plagued aggressive youth to participate in spontaneous play and physical activities. a correctional worker's task is to help him channel his aggression in socially constructive activities. Workers must assist the youth in relating to others through verbal

12. Alan Platon, *The Long View*. New York: Praeger, 1968, p. 19.

expressions. Therefore, it is essential that the approach utilized can achieve the proper integration between his words, feelings, and actions.

Discussions presented in this article pertaining to techniques and skills represent only a few examples that prove to be responsive and relevant to the needs of violent youth. What appears to be more vital and important in working with violent youth is the worker's attitude toward humanity. A healthy attitude will help the violent youth determine what direction to assume in channeling his aggression in immediate as well as future situations. Correctional workers have formerly been reluctant to recognize themselves as authority figures who have the responsibility to exercise limits. Yet therapeutic limit setting seems to be the most indispensable ingredient through which the violent youth is led to believe that a correctional worker's caring for him is more than just befriending him. A correctional worker cares enough to help him set a limit which, although it can potentially jeopardize his existing relationship with the worker, can be conducive to his making an aggression transition from destructive to constructive behavior. The opportunity available for a correctional worker to help the violent youth is more than just helping a young person set limits. He also is the emotional nurturer, information giver, advocate, and live model with whom a violent youngster can experience genuine love and concern, and whom a violent youngster can emulate to become self-actualized.

PART III

WEAPONS AND ARTIFACTS

There is presently much interest in the possibility that spacecraft arrived on this planet thousands of years ago and established advanced civilizations. The brain surgery of the Incas of Peru had a higher success rate than is possible even today. We can examine Incan skulls which show as many as four operations, often over areas of the brain which are so sensitive that neurosurgeons today hesitate to explore them. We have the skulls, the tools the Incas used in the operations, and we have the ability to determine whether the operations were successful. While Peruvian brain surgery may not seem related to juvenile terrorism, I see a very significant relationship; the artifacts of a culture allow us insight into that culture. "Light Bulbs and Lighter Fluid" and "Neighborhood Nonsense: The Street War" illustrate that we can examine the very artifacts of our juvenile gangs to gain a better understanding of their behavior. The article by Dr. Tobias and Thomas LaBlanc, "Malicious Destruction Of Property In The Suburbs — 1975" graphically demonstrates to the reader that gang terrorism and violence is not confined to the urban ghetto. When the suburbanite fled the urban environment, he brought with him the potential for violent acts of malicious destruction in his newly civilized community. That destruction is both a real social problem and a significant economic drain on the society. If the suburban homeowner is ever to be free of this parasite, he must be aware of the problem and then be willing to join with his fellows to do something about that problem. The article, "Graffitti and the Adolescent Personality" by Dr. Pete Peretti, Richard Carter and Betty McClinton suggests a new avenue in the diagnosis of the gang personality. By analyzing

61

the graffitti on bathroom walls, we can broaden our knowledge of what permeates the juvenile mind, and an effective preventative program may be implemented to avert the acting-out of his violence on society. The graffiti on the walls of cave men allowed us the opportunity to study their daily habits. We are aware of the Inca's neurosurgical ability from their skeletal remains. We must use today's artifacts to study the problems of today. We cannot afford to wait 10,000 years to study a social problem of today. If we are to avoid the plight of the Incas — extinction — we must heed the artifacts of today to build a stronger society for tomorrow.

LIGHT BULBS AND LIGHTER FLUID

Regardless of their specific interests or tendencies, all gangs appear to share the contention that their cause will profit faster by bloodshed, disorder and violence, rather than by more conventional change mechanisms. They commit every sort of crime, from bombings to selected "drive-by" shootings. Some of the more sophisticated terrorists probably possess missiles which are shoulder-launched, commonly called "Red-eye missiles," and now the possibility of terrorist possession of nuclear weaponry poses a serious threat to our future safety. Whether we are talking about the "Crips," a youth gang primarily active in Los Angeles on and around school grounds, the Hell's Angels, the Ku Klux Klan, the Puerto Rican Socialist Party, the New World Liberation Army, or prison gangs, one fact remains the same: they all have weapons as a common aspect of their insidious war with the rest of the world.

What are the reasons for their use of weaponry? This question probably goes through the minds of many school teachers and administrators, police officers, legislators, and military officials daily. Possibly, the following information will prove helpful to you, the reader, in understanding why gangs use weapons.

Probably the foremost reason for their use of weapons is

simply that these individuals pose a threat to others and, knowing this, often carry and use weapons defensively as opposed to offensively. Most terrorists are "at war" with someone all the time. School-age individuals associated with local youth gangs or bikers warring against other bikers believe they must arm themselves against their declared foes.

A second reason for the tremendous use of weapons is that weapons get attention, i.e. good press. When a bomb detonates, a significantly greater number of people hear about it as opposed to the number who hear some particular group's spokesman flapping his or her jaws to garner support for their cause.

Thirdly, as a nation, we are an extremely tolerant people. We seem to have a high tolerance for violence. We expect our representatives to talk a hard line on violence, but legislation wanes to control weaponry through the mails, over the store counters, and so forth. We choose to believe, however, that people will not use weapons in an unsportsman-like fashion, or at least not so openly. As long as weapons can make noise, attract attention, injure and kill, they will be used. As a society then, we tolerate to a point a certain amount of violence. However, we have different levels of tolerance, relative to the actors involved.

Let's look a bit closer at who is using what weapons. The separation between various types of armament helps us better understand the gradations of seriousness from a local to a national and international basis and assist in clearly defining, "Who's probably got what?"

For example, street gangs have for some years now used hand guns. The convenience they afford, as well as the types of crimes street gangs commit, readily explain why hand guns are so ideal. When I visited Los Angeles, my first confrontation with street gangs left me terrified. I quickly came to feel that of the 40 million hand guns that exist in the United States, the lion's share must have been distributed in Los Angeles. I talked with no less than thirty gang members that were "packing a piece." That was in one evening while I was on patrol with an undercover police officer. The weapons ranged from small .22 caliber pistols to the more sophisticated police .38 revolvers and .45 automatics. One youth said that many times they would "rip-off the Man," that is, steal from a police officer to secure a weapon. I doubted him and later was able to verify that this was often the case. The Los Angeles Police Department, no discredit intended, reported that many of their officers lost their guns while on duty and that most have never been recovered. A large number of youngsters reported borrowing guns from home. I was prompted to ask, "With permission?" One kid replied, "My old man and brother got guns, now I gotta gun. The only thing is my mother cries everytime she sees me with it. I can use it though. I could blow your ass away if I wanted." I assured him that I believed him and cautioned him not to pursue the matter. The younger gang members, usually ages eight to ten, did not carry guns generally. Due to their size and age, they were easy prey for older gang members to rip off. However, they were armed. They favored the carrying of knives and, from my observations, they could use them.

Most knives I saw were of the pocket type; some, however, were home-made or manufactured in industrial arts classes in local high schools on the sly. I did come into contact with a few stilettos, commonly confused with switchblades and dirks. Stilettos differ, however, because the wrist is used to release the blade-holding mechanism rather than a button. The blade then swings out like a straight razor. For the reader's interest, push-button knives are no longer the weapon of choice. They are out-dated and hardly function as well as a gun. Gangs today prefer to use guns in their pursuit of criminal activities—drug dealing, robbery, assault or extortion.

I also found that youth gangs often make use of certain narcotics or dangerous drugs in order to "O.D.", or overdose their victims. Phencyclidine, commonly referred to on the street as PCP, "angel dust," "dust," "hog," "LBJ," and "wonder," has been used to set up victims for assault, robbery and even homocide. PCP is usually sold as an illicit drug and appears in crystalline form. It is extremely inexpensive to make and is in high demand on the street. It is often sold regularly as cocaine, mescaline, and even LSD, although the use of LSD is seen to be slowing dramatically by drug enforcement officers. PCP can be used to lace other illicit drugs (e.g. sprinkled on marijuana before smoking). It may be inhaled or "snorted" or sniffed directly into the nostrils, or it may be taken orally in tablet form or injected in solution. Gangs either sell to their victims or sell to other kids who do their dealing for them. The potential victim under the influence of PCP initially experiences a relaxing euphoria leading to a loss of contact with sensory perception and, in quantities in excess of ten milligrams, experiences a distortion as to time, place, and personal awareness. It is at this point that the victim is most vulnerable to the gang. Young women have been gang-raped and beaten. Many young women and men report having been robbed but they don't know or remember how it happened. PCP, with its amnesia-like properties, can be a strategic street weapon. It is proving to be so as the number of victims whose urine confirms their ingestion of phencyclidine increases. A myriad of other drugs are used in the same way, but at this time, PCP is being used at a ratio of ten to one, in my estimation. Street gangs, as well as outlaw bikers, realize the potential of PCP.

Presently, bikers, with very few exceptions, still use shotguns and rifles in their criminal activities. They also make good use of explosives. At the time of this writing, investigations are on-going into the deaths of two gang members recently murdered in a flurry of biker feuds in San Diego County. While their bodies lie in repose, the mortuary was bombed. Rival gang members are suspected to be responsible for this bombing. This speculation has been corroborated by the seizure of explosive devices acquired during local raids on biker residences by law enforcement agencies. Further, an explosive device was found in a vehicle being serviced at a car dealer. This device was tied to earlier investigations involving bikers. The bikers' use of explosives is dramatic and, because some have had military training in demolitions, they are relatively proficient. Their explosives consist primarily of dynamite and home-made concoctions.

They acquire many of their manufacturing techniques from sources such as U.S. Army Special Forces training manuals, CIA training manuals, often *The Anarchist Cookbook* and various publications available from the U.S. Government Printing Office. With the availability of "How to" publications on clandestine explosives, it's a wonder we don't have more bombings each year than are presently reported.

Political terrorists might be called the vanguard in weapons' usage. They continue to succeed at startling the entire world with their daring revolutionary acts of seige, hijacking and bombing. Terrorists of this type enjoy ultimate success by wreaking havoc with the authorities and the general public.

Not unlike the behavioral "primal scene," wherein a child seems to vacillate between fear and excitement at watching a parent disrobe, the terrorist lives out his fantasized fear and excitement episode through the use of weapons and clandestine incendiary devices. Any child's initial stimulation to sensory deprivation, for instance his reaction to a fight between his parents, or his watching his parents' sexual activity, may transcend into the later use of terrorist tactics. The child who does not move out of the fear/excitement stage may live the remainder of his life reverting to that initial experience. This experience may be the ideal breeding ground for a terrorist culture.

Terrorists also tend to copy others' provocations. Terrorist's acts are copied over and over, decade after decade. They really do not differ substantially when taken in an historical context. The terrorist seeks out those who are like him. He begins his mental conditioning process. He spearheads the collection and storage of weaponry. He attracts attention to his cause by bomb threats, hijacking threats, cross burnings, or other newsworthy events. He evolves from thinking about other *provocateurs'* actions to exemplification of those violent acts for his own cause.

Most terrorists seem to have an emotional disassociation with bombings, in that they detach themselves from the victims. It is for this reason that bombings by terrorists are more frequent than armed confrontations. With bombs, there is no physical evidence. The terrorist need not be nearby, and bombs are more effective in gaining attention than many other kinds of weapons. Bombs are also considered the work of professional demolition personnel — i.e. experts — therefore, through their use the terrorist organization can gain even greater notoriety. A simple explosion takes only fuel and an oxidizer, but to the unwary public a bombing incident is held in much higher regard than other types of assaults. If one has some nitrate — say from lawn fertilizers at $6.00 for a fifty-pound bag — and a quart of acetone or model airplane fuel, both found at hardware stores, he has a bomb. The public, however, unaware of the ease with which bombs can be made, continues to hold bombers in awe. That may account for part of the recent increase in bombings.

Terrorists can also build missile devices and now do so. Some have gone so far as to steal such sophisticated weapons as the "Red-eye" missile. This missile is heat-seeking, shoulder-launched, and has a range of about 10,000 feet. That is two miles with accuracy. Commercial airlines are now vulnerable to more than just hijackings.

With twentieth century technology the urban guerrilla today, as in the past, will continue to arm himself, train himself, organize his comrades, and carry out his attacks with commando-like accuracy. A recent communique from the New World Liberation Front stated that their bombings would continue. The Red Army in West Germany has put military and civilian authorities on alert by threatening to sabotage Lufthansa's jet liners. The Baader-Meinhof urban terrorists have even gone so far as to set up a central clearing house for attacks within the confines of the Stuttgart-Stammhein prison, where it is a known fact that they also have a cache of weapons and explosives.

Arms and explosives can be camouflaged. One example is best termed a "light bulb bomb." The specific incandescent light bulb used is normally a 100 to 150 watt bulb. A small hole is made near the base of the bulb just above the metal threading. The bulb is then filled with either gun powder or lighter fluid. Straight pins or small finishing nails are then added. The hole is sealed with glue, bubble gum, or even fingernail polish. The bulb is then screwed into the socket with the light switch in the off position. When the light is turned on, the detonated powder or flaming liquid blasts the projectiles throughout the room. One expert in the area of explosives estimated that the velocity of the pins or nails could exceed 1,400 feet per second. Imagine the damage that would incur in a heavily populated classroom or office.

Military surplus stores have not really done the public any favors; they serve as a supermarket for terrorists, especially stores that sell hand grenades. Mr. Bob Howard, an explosives expert on the West coast, told me a story I feel is worth relating. Surplus hand grenades are purchased empty, minus the fuse and powder. A couple dozen might sell for two dollars. Remove the caps from the grenades and by scraping the inside of the grenades with a wooden popsicle stick enough powder may be collected to fill one grenade. The result is a potential and functional explosive.

Other war surplus or construction items also serve to assist the "do-it-yourself bomber." Detonation cord is a highly explosive item by itself. It can be used to wrap packages which may be sent through the mails to fellow terrorists in other locales — including prisons. Mr. Howard also stated that he had seen explosives with fuses made out of firecrackers, mousetraps, clothespins and flashbulbs. On one occasion he saw a C-4 plastic explosive, generally used by the military, ingeniously made into fake chocolate chip cookies. The whitish colored material had been colored with brown shoe polish and then genuine chocolate chips were added. The recently developed adjustable butane lighter is also excellent in the manufacture of bombs. Even a simple molotov cocktail can have as an ingredient white arsenic. This chemical, on the rag inside the thrown bottle (usually a wine bottle which has thin glass to insure breaking), is potentially more lethal than the gas chamber at any state or federal prison. The average galvanized pipe with threaded ends can easily be turned into a bomb by fueling it with powder, drilling a hole for the fuse, and screwing on caps at each end. The average cost of that pipe bomb is about $2.00.

Beer-can hand weapons are popular and easily manufactured. Pipes filled with rocks, gunpowder and a fuse are popular with street gangs. Sulfuric acid placed in jars is a popular bomb in prison situations. Another example of the urban guerilla's ingenuity is the whistle bomb. When the whistle is blown, the air causes a contact to be made between the ball, the striker, and the explosive. The whistle blows up in the blower's face! Letter bombs, a mere two and one-half ounce envelope full of plastique explosive, are capable of demolishing an average room. One can even find the SX-70 camera's chemical battery a perfect source for explosives.

The aforementioned weapon descriptions are not meant to be a definitive list. We are all inherently unique as is our ability to concoct explosive devices. I have chosen to share some of these items with you as a means of expanding your awareness and hopefully prolonging your lives.

NEIGHBORHOOD NONSENSE: THE STREET WAR

Recently, I made a trip to sixteen large cities within the United States to confirm what has been described in so many recent magazine articles and television specials as The Renaissance of Street Wars. The street war phenomenon, which was talked about with a snicker during the "nifty-fifties," which was glamorized in the Broadway musical *West Side Story,* and is presently acted out on the television screen for our viewing pleasure, still exists. There are two misconceptions about street wars that need to be addressed.

Firstly, "neighborhood nonsense" it is not. As a result of the low profile community relations programs of so many of our metropolitan police departments coupled with the indifference of judges and probation officers, gangs today are considered to be little "play groups" who hang around together. While I was in Cleveland and San Diego, the official law enforcement position was, "We don't have any gangs here!" I must say, contrary to that official pronouncement, both of those cities do have gangs and those gangs do wage wars and commit "drive-by" shootings with regularity. A "drive-by" usually is aimed at a rival gang member, a symbol of authority (such as a teacher or probation officer), or even an unknowing victim not associated in any way with the gang except that he or she makes a nifty target. The act, simply stated, requires one gang member to drive an automobile, while one or two others, armed with weapons, fire from the speeding car at the "hit."

The warring gangs are not local groups of kids involved in a little neighborhood nonsense. They are deadly serious. "Walking your lady," stealing hubcaps, protecting your turf (the local area bounded by certain streets wherein the gang resides), and playing basketball with the police in a vacant lot are not the extent of a gang's activities and is a misleading image of gang life. If anything, this misconception has been the result of news reporters who know very little about the internal makeup and motivations of street gangs, augmented by the police's official dismissal of the entire subject.

I spent four days in one city with the local law enforcement officers. One stated to me: "These kids are a helluva lot worse than the kids ten or twelve years ago." One officer remarked, "I'd love to take down (arrest) a kid for an old-fashioned zip-gun instead of a bomb, believe me." These first-hand observations, with and by officers on the street, allow me the opportunity to make some generalizations about street gangs and their wars.

I found that most youth gangs seem to consist of less than twenty members. Usually the member's position in the gang depends on his or her age, their grade in school, if they are still in school, and the willingness to "do bad." The gangs of today that seem to bounce and shuffle around the streets really spend much of their time intimidating merchants for "protection money." Simply stated, the gang informs the owner: "Pay us or we'll do your store in." Gangs also extort money from children at schools, theaters, or on the

recreation department's grounds. Their standard M.O.—
modus operandi—consists of a group confrontation with their
victim. Their hand guns afford superior fire power and the
gang members often show the seriousness of their demands
by inflicting a minor wound on the victim. One storekeeper in
East Los Angeles told me that he spends thirty dollars weekly
for protection and is assured by the protecting gang that he
will not only be safe from the gang which "protects" him,
but they'll also protect his business from any attack by any
other group. He said, "For $120.00 a month, the insurance is
damn good. I paid nearly that much before the gang of kids
came in on me and I still got robbed. I pay the kids, I got no
trouble." I asked him what that reminded him of and he
replied, "Back east in the thirties." According to other
merchants that made up my rather cursory study, they have
learned to live with the gangs—it's safer.

The make-up of these extortionist youth gangs further
intrigued me when I had the opportunity to visit the "Gang
Activity Section" of Chicago's Police Department. Following
are my observations from that visit.

It seems that gang members, at least in Chicago, organize
because of either fear or peer pressure from other
threatening groups. The members range in age from eight to
the early twenties. The gang hierarchy normally reflects the
age and experiences of the members in that the oldest and
most seasoned gang member secures the leadership
position. Usually one can assume that those leaders have
killed, raped, and or stolen in order to be elevated to that
position. The gangs I observed were usually comprised of
young males; their median age was sixteen to eighteen.
However, I did confront three female gangs which were the
off-shoots of their male counterparts. It also is important to
note that I found a significantly larger number of active
female gang members on the West coast as opposed to on
the East coast. A concluding observation is that the ethnicity
of the gangs, weather conditions, and urban crowding are all
contributing factors in examining modalities and motivations
of gangs.

Further, the members of the various gangs in each of the

cities I visited were usually stereotypical ghetto or *barrio* youngsters. Their families were normally in a state of transition and were usually single-parented. The economic instability of the family, as well as the entire slum jurisdiction in question, had a great deal of influence on the young people. Where I found large social congregations of young people, coupled with high unemployment, poor police community relations, and closed school grounds, I also found a much greater incidence of gang activities. The very tools used by society to defuse gang activities, such as dances or cultural events, also serve as an opportunity for those gangs to meet with the complete approval of their greatest enemy; the general public.

While talking with fire marshals and firemen assigned to fire prevention units, I also found a high correlation between the incidence of fires and an increase in gang criminal activity. In one city I was shocked to find that the firemen were despised as much as the police by the street gangs. One gang member stated to me, "The water pigs, firemen, do some shit to my deal, man. I don't like it! If they do me, I'm gonna do them." That "doing" means some criminal act from harassment to homicide.

Most of the gang's harassment or other criminal activity starts shortly after dark. Their agenda might read something like the following scenario provided by a gang member I chatted with this past summer. "Well, we get high, whip some ass, get some pussy, maybe drink some beer or wine or anything, do some coke (cocaine), and sometimes we get blades out and do a robbery. I poked a dude recently and we stripped his old lady and ganged her." I asked how old the couple was and he replied, "About 50 or 60!" Did they enjoy doing that to those people? "Fuck yes! They're punks; we coulda killed them if we'd wanted to!"

I questioned another kid who was hanging around a small neighborhood store in Philadelphia and got a similar report. "We meet and hang around about six or seven p.m. or sometimes later if somebody's old man or old lady hassles them. We get some beer from some store, you know take it, and get fucked up. I get high really fast so I fight and the dudes I hang with like it. I can fight good. Then we maybe start some fires or something. Once we killed a dude that told us he'd whip our asses. We stabbed him a few times, then shot him. Scared the shit out of the people around here. We get anything we want. We even scared the police. Some of them don't even come around because we'd whip 'em or kill 'em maybe.'' I later spoke with police authorities who denied a good portion of these statements. Of course, as one young officer said, ''It happens but who wants to spread that kind of news. It's a shame how kids are today, a real shame.''

Police have had long-standing methods of dealing with gangs that do little more now to alleviate the problem than they did a few years ago. Half-hearted saturation patrols and the use of field interrogations just force gang activities underground. Special school enforcement units, made up largely or solely of local police officers, only serve to alienate the straight kids. Gangs often out-number police officers in the cities under certain circumstances, so police are naturally ineffective as a preventative force. Police speak of mindless actions by gangs, their weaponry which may be more powerful than conventional police weapons, and their knowledge of how to ''beat the rap'' through the use of legal aid; these are all popular topics in station houses. In many areas of the country, as many as thirty police departments meet monthly to discuss the activities of gangs in neighboring communities. I attended meetings of this sort in Los Angeles where the topic of conversation was homicide. During one year in greater Los Angeles, approximately 112 gang-related homicides occurred. Some of the cases remain open today.

From my experiences with street gangs, I suggest the following steps be taken to eradicate or prevent gang violence or criminal activities. First, law enforcement agencies must stop telling the public, ''There is no problem.'' Law enforcement must secure the assistance of the general public in eradicating the problem. Second, the public must demand that their law enforcement agencies tell them what is wrong and how to correct the situation. The ostrich or reactive approach to law enforcement must be discarded and emphasis on prevention and eradication of violent situations which are generated by the gangs must prevail.

MALICIOUS DESTRUCTION OF PROPERTY IN THE SUBURBS — 1975

Jerry Tobias, Ed.D. and Thomas LaBlanc

Over the past year, malicious destruction of property has been among the top anti-social acts committed by suburban youth. In some areas, it is ranked number one and costs resulting from this misbehavior may well escalate into the thousands, perhaps tens of thousands of dollars.

The act itself is described as: **MALICIOUS DESTRUCTION OF PROPERTY**. (FELONY — Over $100); (MISDEMEANOR — $100 or less)

The offense must be shown to be a willful act, with malice. However, the "malice" need not be shown as directed toward any particular person.

The M.D.P. statute contains many specific charges; those most frequently involving juveniles are as follows:

1) Maliciously destroying or injuring animals and personal property of another.
2) Maliciously breaking down or injuring house, barn, or building of another.
3) Maliciously breaking down or injuring fences or opening gates.
4) Maliciously injuring or destroying trees — fruit, shade or ornamental.

ADOLESCENCE, Vol. XII No. 45, Spring, 1977
  Libra Publishers, Inc., 391 Willets Rd., Roslyn Hts., N.Y. 11577

5) Maliciously injuring or destroying boundary markers, guide posts, light bulbs, telephone poles, billboards, posters, etc.
6) Willfully destroying or injuring tombs and memorials to the dead.
7) Malicious annoying by writing.
8) Malicious injury to library books.
9) Willfully destroying ship, vessel, or boat.
10) Throwing stone or missile at train, motor vehicle, etc.

Consequently, as a result of the size of this problem, 1975 complaints were examined in an effort to gain a clearer picture of this behavior and the young offenders involved. The following facts were extrapolated from the data:

1. Most offenses go unwitnessed and appear to be committed without any malice toward the victim; consequently the vast majority of incidents go into the inactive category of crime classifications due to a lack of investigative leads.

2. However, when an offender was apprehended and this was generally the result of a police vehicle being in the immediate area or an alert citizen, it was a white male in his mid to late teens.

3. It is not an act committed by one youngster; it appears to be a group activity involving two or more young people.

4. Oftentimes a car is used in the perpetration of the act; this may serve two purposes—mobility and a weapon of destruction.

5. Today's offender usually commits multiple acts; that is, he doesn't just damage one piece of property during his "destructive run" but may "hit" several homes.

6. The behavior is even considered a "fun and games" activity by some who along with the writer have developed a special "slanguage" describing their acts. For example:

Jungle Patching—Driving over a suburban lawn and "spinning" the tires to lay a "patch" (rut) on same.
Car Crushing or Stomping—"Walking On" top of and/or

"kicking in" a parked vehicle.

Bombing or Blasting—Blowing up a suburban mail box or school toilet with a "cherry bomb" (fire cracker).

Window Wrecking—The breaking of a school, house or car window with a "BB," marble, brick, or some other missile.

Mail Boxing—Knocking over, ending and/or pulling out mail boxes from the ground.

The Academic "hot seat"—Burning a plastic toilet seat in a school lavatory by placing a piece of Kotex between the seat and bowl and igniting same.

7. Many of those arrested have difficulty in giving a specific reason for their behavior; they indicate that they didn't see it as a crime. It was more of a "kick" or thing to do with their friends; they found it exciting and a challenge without a reason.

8. The majority of offenses were committed on the weekend with Friday and Saturday being the most active days. However, during the summer, week days show an increase in destructive behavior.

9. Most acts are perpetrated at night between 8 p.m. and 2 a.m.

10. Damage ranges from a few dollars (the majority of complaints are $50.00 dollars or less) to as high as several hundred dollars with some reaching into the thousands of dollars (these generally are new houses under construction that have been literally raided by local youngsters).

11. The types of property attacked varied, but for the most part were: (a) private dwellings and property; (b) schools and their grounds; (c) churches; (d) business establishments; (e) personal and real property; and (f) public property.

12. The actual property damaged includes: (a) windows (home, school, and vehicle); (b) landscaping (lawns, trees and bushes); (c) mail boxes; (d) lights (school, yard and street); (e) home accessories and interiors (fences, patio blocks, bird bath, lawn equipment, swimming pool cover, statues, snow shovels, walls, and doors); (f) school property

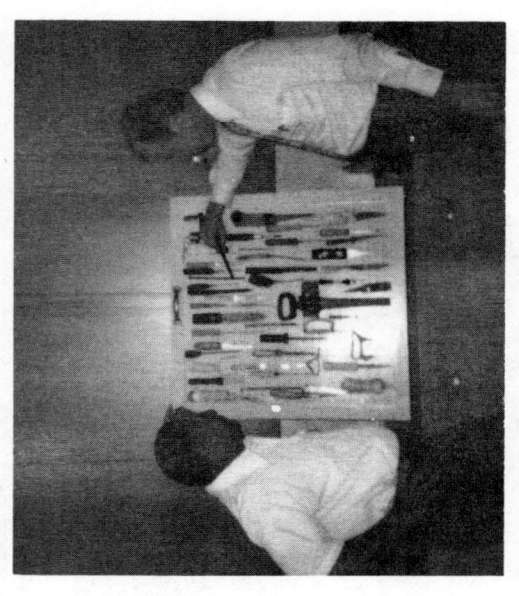

Gang weapons, commonly called "shanks" or "dirks."

Gangs aren't only on the streets but in prison.

An example of the ritualistic fanaticism discussed in "Outlaws on Wheels." The skulls and skeleton are genuine.

Courtesy San Diego County District Attorney's Office

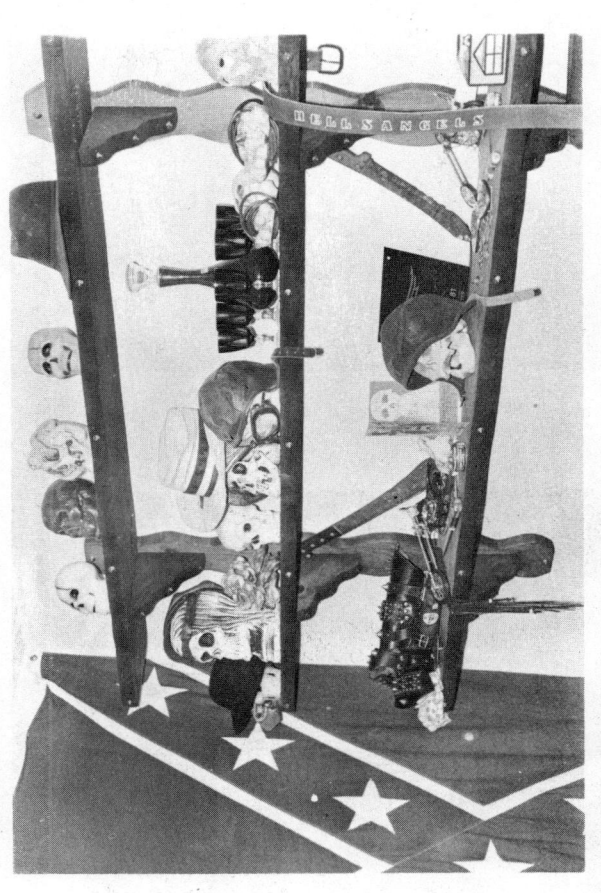

Artifacts such as these are common to the biker world.
Courtesy San Diego County District Attorney's Office

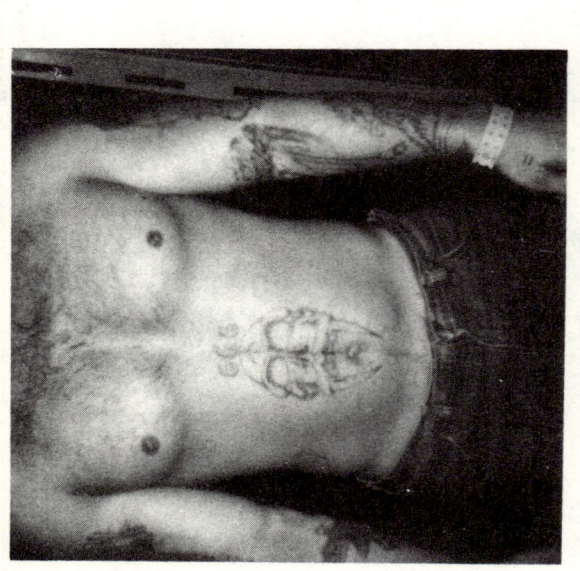

Tatoos "brand" the gang member and identify the gang many times.

"Colors" or "patches" which denote membership in biker gangs.

An armlet, a frequent weapon of outlaws on wheels.
Courtesy San Diego County District Attorney's Office

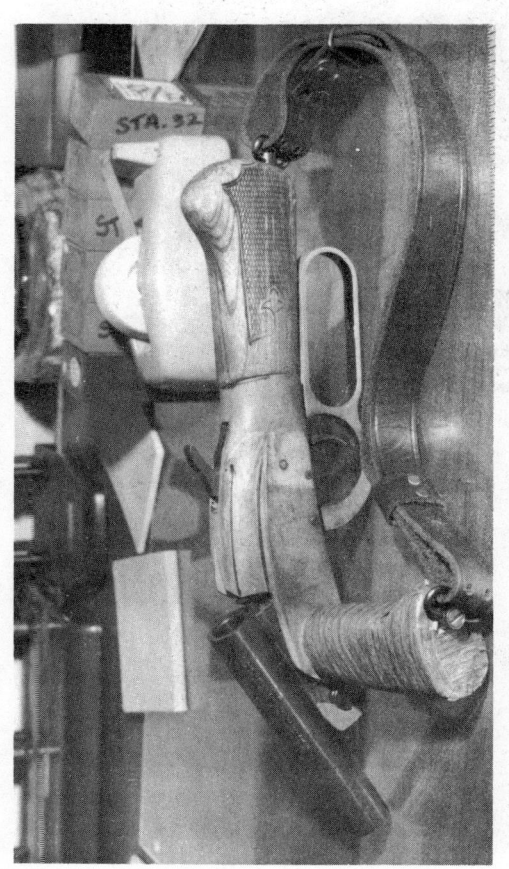

The "gape." A sawed-off 20 gauge gang weapon on a shoulder rig.

A biker funeral.

A biker initiation.

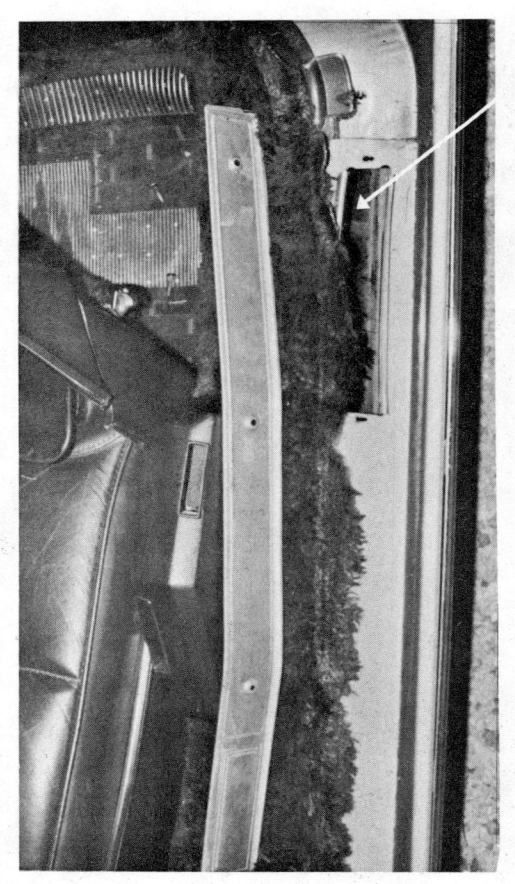

A "dope stash" such as the kickplate is great for evading a police search.

(toilets, toilet seats, doors defaced, lockers, stage curtains ripped, chairs, etc.); (g) exterior of homes (defacing, painting, and egging); public property (street and traffic control signs); (h) vehicles (cars, school buses, fire trucks, and bicycles); and (i) the interior of new homes under construction.

13. The tools or weapons of destruction vary considerably, but for the most part consist of rocks or missiles, BB or pellet guns, knives, beer bottles, a hammer or crow bar, eggs, spray paint or other kinds of paint, snow plow, hands and feet, car, snow balls, tomatoes, explosive devices (fire crackers), sticks, sugar, sand, or dirt, keys, matches, a machette, sling shots, golf clubs, etc.

14. The acts consisted of: (a) burning the church bushes; (b) igniting toilet seats in the school; (c) flushing M-80 fire crackers down school toilets; (d) running over lawns with cars; (e) pulling down and bending mail boxes; (f) carving statements or words on the school doors; (g) breaking windows with marbles projected from sling shots; (h) bending and/or defacing "stop" or "speed limit" signs; (i) placing dirt or sugar in the gas tanks of vehicles; (j) scratching words on automobiles; (k) stomping or kicking in a car (one incident amounts to $750.00); (l) puncturing tires; (m) kicking in the wall board of new homes; (n) ripping the curtains of the school auditorium; (o) breaking all the windows of a home with a golf club; (p) snapping the hood ornaments off luxury cars; (q) throwing snow balls with rocks in them at cars; (r) painting traffic control signs; (s) wrecking bicycles; (t) throwing things into swimming pools; (u) knocking over bird baths and statues; (v) pulling down the school fence, etc.

Malicious destruction of property in the suburbs is not something to be taken lightly. Quite to the contrary, it should be treated as a twentieth century social problem reflecting an epidemic of youthful destructiveness. And this in turn, suggests the existence of an enormous amount of teenage hostility and subsequent uncontrolled aggression vented on the property of others.

I would hope that other communities and professionals will look seriously into this phenomenon so that additional light might be shed on: (1) the actual size of the problem; (2) the characteristics of the youthful offenders; and (3) the causal factors for their involvement. It has been my feeling that other types of anti-social behavior often take precedence over malicious destruction of property and consequently, many tend to underestimate its significance. There must be a re-evaluation and I would hope this effort helps to place the problem in its proper perspective.

GRAFFITI AND ADOLESCENT PERSONALITY

Peter O. Peretti, Ph.D., Richard Carter, and Betty McClinton

ABSTRACT

Graffiti has been studied for many years from many viewpoints. They have been used to explain accounts of people, styles of life, and assumed relationships. The present paper reports an attempt to analyze graffiti as outward manifestations of adolescent personality. Results suggested that different forms of graffiti could be interpreted from five characterizations of early adolescent personality: sexual maturity, self-identity, idealism, iconoclasm, and rebelliousness. Significant differences were found between boys and girls in numbers of inscriptions for each category. Further, the graffiti were analyzed in relation to early adolescent stages of development.

Graffiti are inscriptions of figures, designs, or words on rocks, walls, or sidewalks or the like, or on artifacts made of

ADOLESCENCE, Vol. XII No. 45, Spring 1977
  Libra Publishers, Inc., 391 Willets Rd., Roslyn Hts., N.Y. 11577

plaster, stone, or clay. The singular form is graffito (Reisner and Wechsler, 1974). Some of the earliest research in the field suggested the importance of local graffiti as found in the community to explain accounts of people, styles of life, and assumed relationships (Coulton, 1915, 1928). Graffiti has been used as an anthropological tool to study past and present societies and cultures (Tanzer, 1950; Guarducci, 1958; Pritchard, 1967; Reisner, 1971). Much of the graffiti in these areas has been analyzed and interpreted from viewpoints of social change, turmoil, hardships, and shifting societal conditions among human groups.

The graffitist engages in personal and political views, philosophies, questions, answers, opinions, poems, comedy, satire, dialogues, and advice (Guthrie, 1952; Leary, 1968, 1977; Lindsey, 1973; Winegard, 1974; Kurlansky and Naar, 1974). The nature of the communication may vary, but the graffiti can be studied and evaluated with regard to the graffitist's personality. The material expresses his hopes, fears, desires, hostilities, and frustrations. Through written graffiti, the individual illuminates certain parts of his social and private personalities. (Mendel, 1974; Singer, 1974).

Lindsay (1960) and Kohl (1972) attempted to define the social conditions of the graffitists and their responses to these environments. They maintained that these situations influenced the personalities of the writers and their written expressions. The graffiti might be useful in diagnosing aspects of the personality.

Reisner and Wechsler (1974) and Ingham (1975) stated that much of the graffiti found today was insignificant, banal, trite, ridiculous, and sheer defacement, however, a serious study of these inscriptions has led to further insights into human behavior (Coulton, 1915, 1928; Guarducci, 1958). They can have significance in the analysis of personality (Singer, 1974) and the type of individual writing the material (Mendel, 1974).

Two contrasting views of the graffitists of today are those of Wertham (1974) who maintained a less positive view stating graffiti was part of a widespread vandalism, the mood to destroy, the brutalism that was everywhere; of Goldstein

(1973) who maintained a more positive position stating the graffiti movement was a lot like the rock 'n roll in its prelightened stage. It announces the first genuine teenage culture since the fifties. From either position, certain assumptions are made about personalities of the graffitists. Different personalities are assumed to lead to the production of different forms of graffiti.

The present study was conducted to examine graffiti of youth using a developmental psychological schema. It attempted to analyze graffiti as outward manifestations of adolescent personality. The study explored the possibility that graffiti of different aged youth might be better understood if their analyses were couched within the framework of the growth and development model of personality. It focused, specifically, on the early adolescent personality.

METHOD

Subjects: Seventh and eighth-grade boys and girls, ranging in age from 12 to 16 yrs, from the Bryn Mawr, John Hope, Joshua Kershaw, and Francis Parker Elementary Schools, Chicago, Illinois, where the Ss. Bathrooms were chosen for data-gathering for two reasons: (1) all of the Ss had access to these areas, and (2) all of the Ss had the opportunity to produce graffiti. Collectively, there were 9 bathrooms available for the boys, and 10 bathrooms for the girls. A total of approximately 954 Ss used these facilities. No attempt was made in this study to find out how many of these youth were actively engaged in graffiti production, or how much graffiti was produced by any one person.

Materials: Written inscriptions on the bathroom walls, doors, floors, urinals, or other structures were used in gathering data. They ranged in design from scribblings or doodlings to writings demonstrating clear, precise craftsmanship. Graffiti were produced with pen, pencil, felt marker, paint, chalk, as well as with sharp pointed instruments used to scratch the inscription. They ranged in content along aspects of the adolescent personality. All observable graffiti were copied by the investigators for further analyses. Those found in the boys' bathrooms were kept separate from those found in the girls' facilities.

Operationalization of Terms: The early adolescent personality is characterized by the following terms:

1. *Sexual maturity:* sexual activity; sexual desire; sexual role.

2. *Self-identity:* who am I? what do I value? evaluation of self.

3. *Idealism:* better way of life; personal fulfillment; reform.

4. *Iconoclasm:* attack beliefs; attack institutions; attack authority.

5. *Rebelliousness:* self-independence; self-reliance; self-success.

PROCEDURE

In each of the four schools, the administration was contacted for approval of the study. Further, they were asked to denote those bathrooms used by seventh and eighth-grade students. Each of the school buildings was visited on separate days for data collection, and two schools (Kershaw and Parker) were visited twice.

Both boy and girl bathrooms were visited and examined for graffiti while the Ss were in the classrooms. No visits were made during recess or lunch times when there were large numbers of students using the facilities. All observable sections of the bathrooms were looked at for possible inscriptions. Only written graffiti were of interest, in this study, and pictures, figures, drawings, and designs were not recorded as data. These might be data for some future study. Inscriptions were assumed to be the most expressive and concise of the graffitist, hence, the most representative of his personality. Being verbal data, these graffiti were also less subject to interpretation as would be the case with the nonverbal graffiti discussed above.

Graffiti were collected separately from the boys and girls' washrooms because during the analyses of data similarities and differences in male and female adolescent personalities were to be considered. Whatever the content and nature of the writings, the graffiti were recorded in notebooks.

RESULTS

Graffiti data were grouped by content analysis into one of five categories of the adolescent personality: sexual maturity, self-identity, idealism, iconoclasm, and rebelliousness. Through examination of data, it was found that the writings could be better analyzed and understood by using three sub-categories under each of these classifications. A difference between proportions statistical technique was used to determine significant differences between the total number of inscriptions in each category by sex of S (Table 1). A breakdown of sub-categories can be seen in Table 2. Rank-ordering of the categories and sub-categories was based on frequency of Ss' responses and not based on any preconceived theoretical basis.

Among the elementary school Ss, the greatest number of graffiti were in the category of sexual maturity (42%), followed by self-identity (24%), idealism (14%), iconoclasm (11%), and rebelliousness (9%). Graffiti associated with sexual maturity and self-identity made up about two-thirds of the total number of inscriptions.

TABLE 1

NUMBER OF GRAFFITI RESPONSES FOR BOYS AND GIRLS OF FOUR ELEMENTARY SCHOOLS INDICATING RANK-ORDERING OF CATEGORIES, TOTAL NUMBER OF INSCRIPTIONS OF EACH, AND PERCENTAGE OF SELECTION

Category of Graffiti	Boys N	Boys %	Girls N	Girls %	Totals N	Totals %
1. Sexual Maturity	123	51	71	33	194	42
2. Self-Identity	47	19	62	29	109	24
3. Idealism	14	5	48	22	62	14
4. Iconoclasm	38	16	16	7	54	11
5. Rebelliousness	21	9	19	9	40	9
Totals	243*	100	216*	100	459	100

*Boys averaged 27 graffiti per bathroom; Girls averaged 22

TABLE 2

**NUMBER OF GRAFFITI RESPONSES FOR BOYS AND
GIRLS OF FOUR ELEMENTARY SCHOOLS INCLUDING
RANK-ORDERING OF ITEMS AND PERCENTAGE OF
CHOICE FOR EACH ITEM**

| Graffiti Items in Rank-Order | Subjects | | | | | |
| | Boys | | Girls | | Totals | |
	N	%	N	%	N	%
1. Sexual Maturity	123	100	71	100	194	100
a. sexual activity	58	58	24	34	82	42
b. sexual desire	46	37	32	45	78	40
c. sexual role	19	15	15	21	34	18
2. Self-Identity	47	100	62	100	109	100
a. who am I?	22	47	26	42	48	44
b. what do I value?	16	34	16	26	32	29
c. evaluation of self	9	19	20	32	29	27
3. Idealism	14	100	48	100	62	100
a. better way of life	9	65	21	44	30	48
b. personal fulfillment	2	14	17	35	19	31
c. reform	3	21	10	21	13	21
4. Iconoclasm	38	100	16	100	54	100
a. attack beliefs	18	47	6	38	24	44
b. attack institutions	12	32	6	38	18	33
c. attack authority	8	21	4	24	12	23
5. Rebelliousness	21	100	19	100	40	100
a. self-independence	9	43	8	42	17	42
b. self-reliance	8	38	7	37	15	38
c. self-success	4	19	4	21	8	20

There was a significant difference ($z = 3.69$, p .001) between the graffiti of sexual maturity comparing the boys and girls. The former had the greater number of responses (Table 1). Girls had a significantly greater number of inscriptions, as compared to the boys, in the category of self-identity ($z = 2.25$, p .05), as well as in the area of idealism ($z = 5.15$, p .000). Boys tend to have significantly greater iconoclastic graffiti than girls ($z = 2.65$, p .01).

Both boys and girls had about the same proportion of rebellious graffiti resulting in a lack of significant difference between the two groups of Ss ($z = .056$, p .05).

Sub-categorization, in Table 2, tends to clarify where sex differences can be found in each classification. For males, sexual activity (48%) composed the greatest graffiti, whereas, for females, sexual desire was greatest in inscriptions for sexual maturity. Girls were more concerned than boys (32% as compared to 19%) with the evaluation of self for self-identity. Girls differed from the boys the most significantly in graffiti dealing with idealism. For the sub-category of "better way of life," the differences were 44% and 65%, respectively; for "personal fulfillment," they were 35% and 14%, respectively, and for "reform," they were 21% for both groups. Of note, are the numbers of graffiti in each sex classification — a total of 48 inscriptions for the girls to only 14 for the boys!

Under the iconoclasm category, the boys differed from the girls the most under the sub-category of "attack beliefs" (47% compared to 38%), while both sexes were similar in frequency of graffiti suggesting or referring to rebelliousness. Sex differences can be noted regarding individual rank-ordering of graffiti by sex. For the boys, the ordering is sexual maturity, self-identity, iconoclasm, rebelliousness, and idealism; for the girls, the ordering is sexual maturity, self-identity, idealism, rebelliousness, and iconoclasm (See Tables 1 and 2). It can also be noted that boys averaged 27 graffiti per bathroom, while girls averaged 22 inscriptions (see Table 1).

Tables 3 and 4 present representative graffiti gathered in the study from the boys and girls' bathrooms. Wherever proper names of students or teachers are indicated in the Tables pseudonyms have been used. Graffiti selection for these Tables was based on some of the most pertinent inscriptions for the category and sub-category from those present in the classifications.

TABLE 3

REPRESENTATIVE GRAFFITI SELECTED FROM THE 243 INSCRIPTIONS COLLECTED FROM ELEMENTARY SCHOOL BOYS' BATHROOMS

Graffiti Category and Sub-Categories	Graffiti
1. Sexual Maturity	
a. sexual activity	James fucked Shirley
b. sexual desire	I want to fuck Carol
c. sexual role	Boys fuck and girls suck
2. Self-Identity	
a. who am I?	I'm a cock sucker
b. what do I value?	School is shit
c. evaluation of self	I'm good with Janice
3. Idealism	
a. better way of life	There got to be something better than going to school
b. personal fulfillment	I like graduating
c. reform	Nixon was a queer and Ford is a dear
4. Iconoclasm	
a. attack beliefs	Religion is shit, fucking is where it's at
b. attack institutions	Schools' suck
c. attack authority	Miss Johnson (sic) is a bitch
5. Rebelliousness	
a. self-independence	Fuck "em" all, I'll do it myself
b. self-reliance	No girl can do what I can
c. self-success	I'll show them when I get out of here

TABLE 4

REPRESENTATIVE GRAFFITI SELECTED FROM THE 216 INSCRIPTIONS COLLECTED FROM ELEMENTARY SCHOOL GIRLS' BATHROOMS

Graffiti Category and Sub-Categories	Graffiti
1. Sexual Maturity	
a. sexual activity	Pam and Mark make it with fucking
b. sexual desire	I want John to kiss my twat
c. sexual role	Girls suck dick
2. Self-Identity	
a. who am I?	I'm a lesbian
b. what do I value?	I like guys who are honest
c. evaluation of self	I'd never fuck anybody unless I really liked them
3. Idealism	
a. better way of life	Things will be better when I grow up
b. personal fulfillment	If you've ever been fucked by your boyfriend just right, then you know what Heaven is like
c. reform	Politicians should have their asses kicked
4. Iconoclasm	
a. attack beliefs	Religion is for the birds
b. attack institutions	All schools are bullshit
c. attack authority	Mr. Keller is a no good rotten son-of-a-bitch
5. Rebelliousness	
a. self-independence	I can do it all
b. self-reliance	I do my own thing
c. self-success	I'm happy with me

CONCLUSIONS AND DISCUSSION

Graffiti can be used in the analysis of the adolescent personality. Its inscriptions can be considered to be outward manifestations of the personality of the graffitist. By gathering graffiti at different age and sex levels of Ss, their analyses could lead to increased understanding of youthful personalities along a developmental continuum. Although the present study focused on the early adolescent personality, future studies might consider other ages and stages of human development such as, early childhood, middle childhood, later childhood, and the like.

For the early adolescent personality, the most frequent graffiti dealt with adolescent sexuality. The personality of the youth at this stage of life seems to be involved with a sexual awakening. Biological development of sex organs facilitates sexual maturity and enhances a self and other sex awareness for the youngsters. Both the boys and girls had their greatest number of sub-category responses in "sexual activity," collectively, therefore, it might be concluded that the adolescent personality, regardless of sex of S, includes interest in sexual activity and experience. The interest is not the same for boys and girls. When looking at the sub-categories of "sexual maturity," "sexual activity" was most frequent graffiti for boys, while "sexual desire" was most frequent graffiti for girls. Therefore, the male, early adolescent personality tends more toward the activity of sex, while the female personality tends more toward the sexual desire. The least number of graffiti, for both sexes dealing with "sexual maturity," were those seemingly involved with the "sexual role." Lack of intensity and specificity in this area might be due to the recent awakening in sexuality. Role considerations might result in greater graffiti within the next few years — in later adolescence or early adulthood.

The category of "self-identity" had the second most frequent graffiti for both boys and girls. This suggests a central aspect of the adolescent personality involving a sense of self in relation to others and to the world. Each youth has a self-awareness and tries to find out where he fits as an individual and as a social person. Data indicated the girls have their most frequent graffiti in the sub-category of "who am I" as did the boys. At this stage of development, both sexes have to come to terms with a "new" body, and with "new" potentials for feeling and acting. Corresponding changes influence the personality and would influence future forms of graffiti. The sub-category of "evaluation of self" had the second greatest graffiti for girls, but was the least in rank-order for boys. Psychologically, this could mean the female personality is much more aware and sensitive to how she thinks about herself. Adolescent girls tend to be more self-conscious, modest, and shy than boys. Graffiti concerned with "what do I value" was second most frequently found for boys in this group, while they were least frequently found for girls. This might suggest that the male adolescent personality is somewhat stronger in its search for independence, self-reliance, and status with peers than the female. He seeks and holds values which enhances achieving these goals. Girls might be more prone to conform to peer group values without having to question values as much as the boys.

For the female, early adolescent personality, "idealism" was the third most frequently found graffiti, and it was the least frequently found for males. These data suggest girls are more concerned with "ideals" at this age and stage than are the boys. Both the boys and girls had the greatest number of sub-category responses in "better way of life." Regardless of sex, the adolescents are involved in losing old illusions about life and building new ones to take their place. The personalities are conscious of and troubled by a sense of difference between what seems to be and what is. They try to strive toward the "better way," whatevever this might be for them. Graffiti of "personal fulfillment" was the second most female sub-category, whereas it was the least frequent for males. Somewhat faster biological development for girls, as compared to the boys at this stage, could suggest they might be able to fulfill more of their desires, ambitions, and the like than the latter. At this stage, girls tend to become more involved with others than do boys, hence "personal fulfillment" has a better probability of being met. "Reform"

graffiti was the least frequent for both boys and girls. This could suggest that the early adolescent personality, although seemingly seeking a "better way of life," nevertheless, is slow to give up old illusions and ideals in the search for new ones. The adolescent seeks new ways of doing things, new ideas, and new ideals, however, since he is not quite sure which of these new aspects are best for himself, the interest in reform is not as great as if the goals were simple and clear.

Graffiti related to "iconoclasm" were third in the boys' frequency of inscriptions and last or fifth for the girls. The male adolescent personality tends to be more aggressive toward tradition and traditional beliefs than the female. The sub-category of "attack beliefs" had the greatest number of male writings, while this one and that of "attack institutions" were tied for most graffiti of the girls. As both sexes had more graffiti on the beliefs, it can be concluded that the adolescent personality, in early adolescence, becomes disillusioned with everyday adult activities, bureaucratic mechanization, and institutional structures. It strives to attack traditional beliefs and recreate a "better" world. Among early adolescents, converts, reformers, and philan-thropists would not be unusual social types. Boys and girls had the least frequent "attack authority" graffiti. It might be concluded that the iconoclasm is more directed toward structures and functions rather than toward people. Conflicts with authority figures, particularly parents, do occur, however, adolescents and their parents (as well as other authority figures) spend most of their time with each other getting along harmoniously.

Collectively among the Graffiti categories that of rebel-liousness appeared the least frequently. By sex of S, it was fourth in inscription frequency for both boys and girls. This rank-order suggests that although early adolescents do rebel, their frequency of occurrence is not as great as is that of other personality factors (the others in the study). It is probably more noted due to its greater social undesirability and acceptance as compared to them. The sub-category of "self-independence" had the most graffiti for both sexes. Due to early adolescent personality changes, the youth

becomes frustrated, humiliated, resentful, and sullen. He seeks to "do his (her) own thing." In these strivings, the youngsters often find that they do need other people and are not totally self-sufficient. The independent-dependent conflict needs resolution which carries beyond this age and stage. "Self-reliance," as the second most frequent graffiti, follows the striving for independence. Both boys and girls had this as second in inscriptions suggesting a developmental trend—independence followed and/or associated with self-reliance. The least frequent graffiti, for both sexes, were those of "self-success." This could suggest that early adolescence is somewhat too early in developmental growth for frequent considerations of self-success. The youngsters, at this stage, are still trying to find out about themselves, and cannot really evaluate "success" or "failure" until they find themselves to use for a base measure. With the affirmation of self-identity, the adolescent in future years can attempt to measure "self-success" in terms of how he measures up to what he thinks he is at that time.

REFERENCES

Coulton, G.G. *Mediaeval Graffiti*. Proceedings of the Cambridge Antiquarian Society, Cambridge, England, 1915.

Coulton, G.G. *Art and the Reformation*. London: Oxford University Press, 1928.

Goldstein, R. "Graffiti," *New York Magazine,* March 26, 1973, 13.

PART IV

EXPECTATIONS AND PROGNOSIS

"A majority of experts predicts an eventual increase in terrorist activity and an escalation of its intensity."

This quotation is from the Introduction to the *Report of the Task Force on Disorders and Terrorism,* which is reprinted here for the readers' information. This *Report* was funded by the U.S. Department of Justice, Law Enforcement Assistance Administration. The members were prominent citizens from all walks of life. They found terrorism to be a significant problem but one which could only be solved with the complete cooperation of the public. The criminal justice system has been notoriously, by public demand I must add, an agency that responds. They step in after an incident takes place. If the American public wishes them to focus their efforts on prevention rather than reaction, then that public must make those desires known and enacted through their representative system of government. The Justice Department knows how to diminish terrorist events. They can only implement that information if they are allowed to do so by public mandate.

"NATURE AND EXTENT OF THE PROBLEMS [OF TERRORISM AND CIVIL DISORDERS] IN CONTEMPORARY AMERICA."

The two concerns of this report—disorders and terrorism—have both common characteristics and specific differences. Both are forms of extraordinary violence that disrupt the civil peace; both originate in some form of social excitement, discontent, and unrest; both can engender massive fear in the community. Disorders and terrorism constitute — in varying forms and degree — violent attacks upon the established order of society. However, the focus, direction, application, and purpose of the terror are different.

Civil disorders are manifestations of exuberance, discontent, or disapproval on the part of a substantial segment of a community. They do not necessarily have political overtones, and they may arise simply from excessive stimulation during an ordinary event, such as a rock concert or football game. In many cases, disorders are haphazard happenings rather than systematically staged and directed expressions of social or political violence. They are collective discharges of explosive rage which can find no outlet other than angry, hostile, fear-generating behavior — ranging from abusive language to large-scale destruction of life and property.

The acts of extraordinary violence characterized as terrorism in this report are the work of a comparatively small number of malcontents or dissidents who, their rhetoric notwithstanding, threaten the security of the entire community. Acts of terrorism are planned in advance, although their execution may be a matter of sudden opportunity. To be effective, terrorism requires a calculated manipulation of the community to which its message is addressed. In the case of civil disorders, the terror generated is incidental and spontaneous, though not always unexpected. In the case of terrorism, on the other hand, the fear is deliberate; it is the very purpose of the violent activity. Civil disorders, and the fear and disruption incidental to them, are ripe for exploitation by the same dissidents responsible for acts of terrorism. When such exploitation takes place, the purpose is the same: the disruption of normal political and social life. Whatever the immediate or ulterior objective of the terrorist, his prospects for success depend to a large extent upon the involvement of the community in his purposes. Terrorism without an audience is an exercise in futility; in this respect, terrorism is as much a collective phenomenon as the mass disorder.

Mass disorders and terrorism, as manifested in the United States, have a distinctive, common quality that Hofstadter has described [p. 10]:

An arresting fact about American violence, and one of the keys to understanding of its history, is that very little of it has been insurrectionary. Most of our violence has taken the form of action by one group of citizens against another group, rather than by citizens against the State.

Disorders in the United States have been no less frightening or bloody than those in other countries, but they have been distinctively different. Mass protest in this country—even when organized on a massive scale—has been directed at modifying our system of government, not at overthrowing it. All responses to civil disturbances should take this fact into account. Similarly, terrorism never developed into advanced guerrilla warfare in the United States as it has elsewhere. It is certainly not that terrorists wish to preserve the American way of life, but that their efforts have been too limited, too unpopular, and too disorganized to seriously affect it.

As disturbing as these occurrences have been for the community, they have never constituted a serious threat to the Nation's government or to the established order of American society. The nature of American society enables it to absorb a great deal of undifferentiated violence without real damage to its political structure or the prospect of a true revolution. This is an important consideration in any valid assessment of the trend of extraordinary violence and the severity of the terroristic threat.

CIVIL DISORDERS

Civil disorders are a form of collective violence interfering with the peace, security, and normal functioning of the community. They are public in character even though, like institutional disorders, they may take place in a restricted setting. Although on occasion they begin with surprising suddenness and develop with alarming speed and intensity, mass disorders are always outgrowths of their particular social context. Indications of such occurrences, though often ignored at the time, can be clearly detected by hindsight. Civil disorders can develop out of legitimate expressions of protest, lawfully organized and conducted. Many such are symptomatic of deep-seated tensions in community relationships; when a precipitating event occurs, these tensions erupt into violence. The immediate, official response to disorder must restore order and permit the normal functioning of the community; only a long-range strategy can remove the root causes of disorder and insure that it will not recur when emergency constraints have been lifted.

These general observations apply to all civil disorders whatever their nature and origin. They apply equally to massive, urban uprisings, such as those examined in 1968 by the National Commission on Civil Disorders, and to small-scale prison riots. More attention must be paid to the signs of potential disorders; prompt and effective steps must be taken to avoid them. It is not sufficient to simply prepare for their consequences. Hannah Arendt reminded us that [p. 7]:

Events, by definition, are occurrences that interrupt routine processes and routine procedures; only in a world in which nothing of importance ever happens could the futurologists' dream come true. Predictions of the future are never anything but projections of present automatic processes and procedures, that is, of occurrences that are likely to come to pass if men do not act and if nothing unexpected happens; every action, for better or worse, and every accident necessarily destroys the whole pattern in whose frame the prediction moves and where it finds its evidence.

There is considerable potential for disorders of all kinds in a pluralistic society; history teaches that their occurrence is neither random nor truly spontaneous. Once a pattern of disorder has been identified, proper attention to its indicators becomes an important exercise in practical politics. Van den Haag's observation that [p. 97] "Riots usually occur not

94

despite, but because of rapid improvements. Improvements, at least in the initial stages tend to intensify dissatisfactions and mobilize preexisting resentments . . ." seems to be applicable to the American experience. Although each disorder has its own general and specific origins — which must be detected and understood so as to permit proper response — civil disorders in general must be regarded as endemic to our society. Their intensity, duration, and extent could indicate a widespread problem, but the phenomenon itself should not be viewed either as evidence of social disintegration or the work of foreign subversive influences. Civil disorders of the type discussed in this report should be seen for what they are: periodic eruptions of social discontent. There is no "best" way to deal with them, but we must prevent their exploitation by antisocial elements. Responses to disorders should be designed accordingly.

It would be tempting to dismiss the serious disorders of the 1960's as nonrecurrent products of a particularly turbulent era, of a nation divided by deep ideological issues during a period of rapid social transformation. That they were so successfully contained without serious harm to the essential fabric of American society is still cause for wonder and gratitude. However, it is ominous that despite the period of calm that has ensued — perhaps even because of it — so little has been done to address the underlying causes of the social discontent that these mass protests proclaimed. The precipitating factors of the conflict have disappeared, and because of their topical nature may never emerge in exactly the same form. However, because the deeper dissatisfactions remain, there is always a likelihood that new controversies and compelling issues may one day precipitate other outbursts of violence.

We cannot afford to ignore the underlying causes of civil disorders during this period of relative calm. The urban crisis is far from being resolved; in many ways, the state of the great cities is more desperate than it was during the most serious riots of the 1960's. An unstable economic situation has forced substantial curtailment of public services in many cities and caused a general deterioration in the quality of life for the poorer classes. Crimes of violence, damaging to both criminal and victim, continue at an unacceptably high level. Unemployment has risen markedly, and job opportunities for the disadvantaged have dwindled. These facts may well have contributed to the present quiescence. But this is a false calm, and we must see in the current social situation an accumulation of trouble for the future. There will surely come a time when once again socioeconomic conditions will generate violent reactions. It is important that we be prepared to deal with such future disorders; it is more important that we reflect now on what is necessary to avoid the tragedy, the recriminations, the inevitable commissions of inquiry, and, in the oft-quoted words of Kenneth Clark, "[The] same moving picture shown over and over again, the same analysis, the same recommendations, and the same inaction."

For all our experience of civil disorders, we are woefully lacking in reliable data about them that would enable us to make sensible projections for the future. Reporting, collection, and storage of such important information are currently so unreliable that many comments on these matters are mere conjecture. It may be too late to undertake the monumental task of accurately reconstructing even the most violent disorders of the last decade. However, we should be prepared to preserve a comprehensive record of future occurrences. We need not only an accurate count of incidents as they take place, but also a proper analysis of them within clearly defined categories that would make useful comparisons possible. It is certain that disorders will continue to occur. An important part of our response strategy should be to improve our methods of collection, storage, analysis, and retrieval of data on civil disorders so that our responses might be meaningful and effective.

THE PROBLEMS OF TERRORISM

A fundamental problem for our understanding of terrorism is that of definition. In any useful definition, there is, as Georg Schwarzenberger has observed [p. 72], an essential element of circularity. The term terrorism, as it is frequently employed, is emotive and unspecific. The lack of precision in its use has led some to believe that the concept defies concrete definition within a normative context. Yet Ludwig Wittgenstein reminded us that, "Everything that can be thought at all can be thought clearly. Everything that can be put into words can be put clearly." [Tractatus Logico-Philosophicus, 4.116.]

It is suggested that part of the problem results from our categorization of terrorism as a substantive criminal activity. In fact, terrorism is a technique, a way of engaging in certain types of criminal activity, so as to attain particular ends. For the perpetrator of terroristic crimes, terror — or the sensation of massive, overwhelming fear induced in victims — transcends in importance the criminal activity itself, which is merely the vehicle or instrumentality. Terror is a natural phenomenon; terrorism is the conscious exploitation of it. Terrorism is coercive, designed to manipulate the will of its victims and its larger audience. The great degree of fear is generated by the crime's very nature, by the manner of its perpetration, or by its senselessness, wantonness, or callous indifference to human life. This terrible fear is the source of the terrorist's power and communicates his challenge to society.

Terror is a constituent of many ordinary crimes, either as a normative element, as in robbery or, incidentally, such as in rape. In a robbery, the victim is threatened so that he will relinquish his property; his fear, however great and essential to the criminal's success, is not meant to be an example to others. Similarly, the fear generated by the crime of rape is aimed at overcoming the will of the instant victim, not at the minds or resistance of others. Such crimes may terrify, but they are not terrorism. An act of terrorism, on the other hand, has a purpose similar to general deterrence: the instant victim is less important than the overall effect on a particular group to whom the exemplary act is really addressed. Thus, terrorism, although it has its individual victims, is really an onslaught upon society itself. Any definition of terrorism for the purpose of constructing effective responses to it must bear these considerations in mind.

It is not useful, therefore, merely to enumerate a series of violent, criminal acts or threats that would constitute terroristic behavior; such a definition misses, altogether, the terrorist's true objective. Any law intended to strike at terrorism must address the purpose as well as the instrumentality. Because they have failed to do so, international attempts at definition have substantially failed: viewed in terms of motivation and ends, "what is terrorism to some is heroism to others." [Per M. Cherif Bassiouni, cited in *International Terrorism and Political Crimes.*] Although it is presently an effective bar to any concerted response to international or transnational terrorism, this lack of agreement about terms and criminal policy ought not to frustrate those responsible for this society's responses to acts of terrorism. For the purpose of the present report, no such universality of consensus is needed in order to arrive at working definitions. **Terrorism is a tactic or technique by means of which a violent act or the threat thereof is used for the prime purpose of creating overwhelming fear for coercive purposes.**

POLITICAL TERRORISM

Political terrorism is characterized by: (1) its violent, criminal nature; (2) its impersonal frame of reference; and (3) the primacy of its ulterior objective, which is the dissemination of fear throughout the community for political ends or purposes. **Political terrorism may be defined, therefore, as violent, criminal behavior designed primarily to generate fear in the community, or a substantial segment of it, for political purposes.** Excluded from this definition are acts or threats of a purely personal character and those which are psychopathological and have no intended sociopolitical significance. To illustrate: the killing of a police officer in the ordinary course of a felony, however brutally the act might have been carried out, would not fulfill this definition. The deliberate killing of a police officer, unconnected with the commission of any other crime and having as its object the intimidation of other members of the police force and the community as a whole, would be characterized as an act of political terrorism. A bank robbery intended simply to obtain money would not be an act of political terrorism because of the manner of its execution or the fact that victims were, incidentally, put in fear. It would take on the character of political terrorism only if the perpetrators deliberately engendered fear in the victims for political ends. Even if the crime were intended to finance illegal subversive or revolutionary operations, it would not necessarily assume the nature of a terroristic act.

Kidnaping for ransom, when the only purpose of the kidnaper was private gain, would be excluded from this definition. The skyjacking of a commercial aircraft, by its very nature a terrifying act, would not be an act of political terrorism if the crime were committed for private gain or represented the non-political act of a mentally disturbed person. For each of the examples given, the law is generally comprehensive and severe enough to encompass both the crime itself and any element of terror arising incidentally from it. It is the purpose of the political terrorist, usually manifested in the cruelty or the wantonness of his behavior, that is beyond the scope of ordinary laws. When special laws are enacted for the purpose of sanctioning such behavior with increased severity or authorizing specific responses to it, it is important that the term political terrorism be used with care and precision. It should never be allowed to degenerate through promiscuous use into an automatic label for all violent acts of a terrifying nature.

There are other important reasons for insisting upon definitional clarity. Terrorism is an attention-getting word. Casual or imprecise use of the term engenders a climate of fear and uncertainty that can spread further afield through the popular media. Eventually, a mystique is built up that allows for a reduction of actual violence while fear itself is increased, and the mere threat suffices to achieve the terroristic objective. In terms of efficiency and economy of endeavor, such a development furthers the terrorist's cause. Once an individual or group has succeeded, in the popular idiom, in being labeled as "terrorist," every criminal activity in which it engages tends to be popularly characterized as "terroristic." In this way, the notion of terrorism is propagated, the fear of victimization increases in the community, and a false picture of the dimensions of the problem is created. It is important that any response strategy should deny the terrorist the benefits of careless description.

To the term political terrorism as defined here, we must add other qualifiers for the sake of clear discussion. Domestic, political terrorism refers to violent, criminal acts of terrorism committed by individuals or groups originating within the United States. Ordinarily, these will be residents whose criminal activities are directed at a particular element of the society and whose purposes are related to the country's domestic or foreign interests. Thus, the bombing of a United States bank in New York City by an indigenous group would be an act of domestic terrorism even if it was a protest against the institution's policies overseas. Similarly, an attack by a United States group, such as the Jewish Defense League, on Soviet property or interests within the United States to protest the treatment of Soviet Jewry would be an act of domestic terrorism. Political terrorists who strike at targets in other countries are termed international or transnational terrorists. Examples of this type of activity would be an overseas bombing by an American group, such as the Weather Underground, or the bombing of a target in the United States by the Palestine Liberation Organization. International terrorism is nonterritorial warfare waged for the coercive value of the fear it causes. Countries victimized by these terroristic acts may have no direct connection with the issues at stake, but they are drawn into a struggle as examples or to discourage their normal comity with the political opponent. Political terrorism of this sort is a global phenomenon in which random selection of innocent victims serves to horrify the world, as did the cruel massacre of Christian pilgrims at Lod Airport in 1972.

The increasing alarm with which terrorism is viewed worldwide today is due in large measure to the success of the transnational terrorists. Making full use of modern communications media and taking advantage of the divisions and disagreements among nations, these terrorists have been able to wreak havoc with a substantial degree of impunity. The failure of the Ad Hoc Committee on International Terrorism of the United Nations [General Assembly Official Records, 28th Session, Supplement No. 28, A—9028], to reach a conclusion as to what international terrorism really is must not be allowed to deter this country from taking appropriate measures to protect the lives and property of United States citizens at home and abroad from terroristic attacks.

NONPOLITICAL TERRORISM

Nonpolitical terrorism is a narrowly defined category for the purposes of this report. The word political has been widely construed to include all activities related to violence directed against authority or having as its main purpose the production of social change through violent means.

There is a vast area of true terroristic activity that clearly cannot be termed political, notably that frequently ascribed to the present-day operations of organized crime. This is true terrorism, exhibiting conscious design to create and maintain a high degree of fear for coercive purposes, but the end is individual or collective gain rather than the achievement of a political objective. Unquestionably, such terror may affect society and its patterns of behavior on a considerable scale. Although such terrorism is not the main subject of this report, many of the problems of response to it are similar in nature to those discussed here. Similarly, school vandalism and other terroristic behavior of teenage gangs that is designed in many instances expressly to terrorize a community does not fall within the definition of political terrorism. Although the aggrandizement of fear is achieved, its message is largely unexploited for political ends. Other criminal activity of a manifestly terroristic nature, such as that engaged in by Charles Manson and his followers, is also a form of nonpolitical terrorism. This is a borderline case, but such political elements as were introduced at a late stage seem to have been rationalizations after the fact. The social structure of the groups involved and the objectives they pursued were not of a truly political character, nor was the victims' fear primarily directed toward achievement of social or political change.

Another type of nonpolitical terrorism is the work of mentally disturbed individuals whose terroristic activities are committed in obedience to some internal demand of a psychopathological nature. Examples of this would be Metesky, the "mad bomber" of the 1950's, and the sniper killings of Charles Whitman from the campus tower in Austin, Texas. Such terrorism is discussed in this report with respect to the different responses necessary to counter it, some of which are relevant to handling political terrorists who show symptoms of mental stress or imbalance.

QUASI-TERRORISM

Quasi-terrorism is a description applied in this report to those activities incidental to the commission of crimes of violence that are similar in form and method to true terrorism but which nevertheless lack its essential ingredient. The behavior distinguished here is a synthetic or pseudo terrorism; although it is not the main purpose of the actor to induce terror in the instant victim, he uses the modalities and techniques of the true terrorist and produces similar consequences and reaction. Quasi-terrorism is the use of terroristic techniques or tactics in situations that are not terroristic crimes per se; it is different from common crimes that involve terror for this reason.

The taking of hostages is a prime example of a common terroristic technique that has been adopted by quasi-terrorists. In the true terroristic situation, the victims who are seized and threatened serve as a bargaining counter to coerce authorities to comply with the terrorist's demands. This situation is then exploited for publicity purposes in such a way as to serve the terrorist's ends. It has become increasingly common in recent years for ordinary criminals who have no original terroristic purpose, to take hostages in the course of a conventional crime of violence, such as bank robbery. In such cases, hostages are terrorized and used as bargaining counters either to facilitate the commission of the offense or to avoid the consequences of apprehension.

Quasi-terroristic acts frequently are directed toward other ends, such as the exploitation of a particular situation in the course of a prison riot for protest purposes or to secure freedom in exchange for the lives of the hostages taken. Although it is clear that this cannot be true terrorism according to the criteria established, the techniques and tactics are perfectly imitated and the responses called forth to cope with the phenomenon are essentially the same.

Skyjacking, too, can be a manifestation of true terrorism, as when a transnational terrorist seizes a passenger aircraft in flight to compel a political adversary to accede to his demands, or quasi-terrorism, when the aircraft and hostages are threatened subject to the payment of a ransom for private gain. Although quasi-terrorism is certainly not new, its manifestation is increasing as criminals imitate the more spectacular incidents of true terrorism that have served as recent models. It is significant that the bulk of the American experience has been in the handling of quasi-terrorism, a field in which a variety of response techniques has been tried and tested with a satisfactory degree of success. Many factors present in a situation involving international terrorists are quite different from those inherent in the quasi-terroristic situation and call for different response patterns. This is particularly true with respect to negotiations. The interests involved, the character of the terrorists themselves, and the command structure of the responding agencies will all be untypical compared to the domestic experience, and vastly different from those elements in a quasi-terroristic setting. Caution must, therefore, be exercised in applying the lessons of the one experience to the other.

LIMITED POLITICAL TERRORISM

Political terrorism in its fully developed form is revolutionary in character; whether it is a realistic tactic or not, it has as its purpose the subversion or overthrow of an existing regime. But many incidents of political terrorism have more limited objectives, either to fulfill a specific purpose or because the terrorists know they lack the strength and popular support they need for a larger attack. Paul Wilkinson has called such acts "sub-revolutionary terrorism" and defined them as [p. 120]: "[A]cts of terrorism which are committed for ideological or political motives but which are not part of a concerted campaign to capture control of the State." Clearly terroristic by reason of the technique employed and political objectives, these acts are limited to their particular social context. The execution-style killings ordered by the Spanish Anarchist labor leader Durrutti in reprisal for the killing of his followers is an example of limited political terrorism. The act of the lone terrorist, impelled by essentially private motives to do a public, political act of this sort would be another. Much domestic terrorism is of this type, and the category is important for the distinctions it raises and the differences in response for which it calls. It reminds us, in particular, that not all subversives are terrorists and that not all terrorists are subversive in the sense that they seek the overthrow of the state.

OFFICIAL OR STATE TERRORISM

For the sake of completeness, some mention is necessary here of official or state terrorism. The United Nations Report of the Ad Hoc Committee on International Terrorism said [p. 15]:

In the opinion of several representatives, it was the terrorism of State which constituted the principal causes of individual violence. The opposition between the oppressive policies of a State and the will of a people led the State to use violence and this reciprocally led the people to react by violent means. The terrorism against a State was provoked by a violent action on the part of a State or by a situation of political injustice, economic inequality or social trouble and by the failure of all other means of redress available to the victims. In this connection, specific reference was made as to causes of international terrorism of the repressive acts of colonial, racist, and alien regimes against peoples struggling for their liberation and legitimate right to self-determination, independence and other fundamental freedoms.

There have been, are, and probably always will be, nations whose rule is based upon fear and oppression that reach terroristic proportions. It is not considered pertinent here to criticize or to make value judgments about such regimes. However, much terroristic behavior by individuals and dissident groups is claimed to be a response to the terroristic behavior of such governments. Many incidents of international terrorism are justified by similar claims, and much of the difficulty in reaching international agreement on what to do about terrorism can be traced to these competing contentions. This old anarchist argument, which can clearly be pressed too hard for conviction in many cases, must be seriously addressed because it is now used over an extremely wide range of situations. At one extreme, it is invoked by prison inmates to justify militant resistance to authority; at the other, it can orient domestic terrorist strategy toward actions likely to provoke massive official repression. In the latter case, overreaction is characterized as "Fascist repression" and any incidental disruption of public order is used to justify the very terrorist activity that has caused it.

The Reign of Terror of a truly repressive regime should be distinguished from the occasional acts of terror that may occur even in democratic systems — from pure, unauthorized acts of exasperation committed by state agents through lack of proper supervision or control to those that represent officially sanctioned or condoned overreactions. There is a clear distinction between the systematic terror used by the Nazi regime to hold down the countries of occupied Europe and the occasional excesses committed by the Allied forces. The Reign of Terror is sometimes contrasted as being the official response to what is called the Siege of Terror against the state by subversive or dissident groups. Political terrorism by individuals or groups is then justified as a reaction to repression or self-defense. In particular, wars of national liberation are frequently justified as a reaction to state terrorism. There are clearly great dangers in this type of thinking; it can lead to a philosophical justification of terrorism that is quite unacceptable. The position taken in this report is that no form of terrorism is acceptable as an instrument of political policy.

One related point is of considerable importance for the

purposes of the present report. Acts of serious terrorism, particularly those which constitute an organized campaign of significant proportions will often require a military response. It is extremely easy for such a response to become excessive and brutal, as has happened in Brazil and Uruguay, for example. A military response may be most necessary and can be highly effective, provided it is kept within lawful bounds and is perceived by the community as being limited in this way. It must never be allowed to degenerate, through lack of discipline or individual excesses, into an excuse for further acts of terror by dissidents; neither must it be allowed to develop into systematic state terrorism condoned by the authorities.

ACTS AND THREATS

Terrorism may be constituted by either acts or threats. From the time of the early anarchists, the ''deed'' assumed a symbolic importance almost as great as the practical consequences of the act itself. For example, the assassination of a hated authority figure as a manifestation of terrorist power embodied the ability to strike at even the most powerful adversaries and the capacity to generate fear and insecurity in society as a whole, and gave powerful encouragement to those of similar persuasion. Terroristic acts encourage imitators and give rise to spontaneous, informal association in common exultation and vicarious participation in the deed; it can be demonstration, stimulus, and model. By attracting publicity, the act fulfills the terrorist's prime purpose of disseminating a message throughout the community, what Regis Debray terms ''armed propaganda.'' [*Revolution in the Revolution?*] The act can be either an announcement of what is to come or a reinforcement of what has already taken place. Some terroristic acts are in themselves a threat or warning, for example, the flaming Ku Klux Klan crosses. Terroristic threats represent an economy of terroristic effort, a capitalizing on an established reputation for fear-generating violence. Threats maximize the effort of a very small, violent group and create an impression of power sufficient for an effective challenge to established authority. Threats give substance to terrorists' power and elevate the level of fear created by it.

The principal problem in designing responses to terroristic threats is assessing their credibility. As a general rule, all threats must be taken seriously. This imposes a considerable strain upon the system's resources, especially in times of crisis, and is complicated by the problem of contagion and consequent "crank calls" that often succeed a genuine terrorist act. All this is part of the War of Nerves that the true terrorist wages. In the words of Marighella, the deceased Brazilian terrorist: "The object of the war of nerves is to misinform, spreading lies among the authorities, in which everyone can participate, thus creating an air of nervousness, discredit, insecurity, uncertainty, and concern on the part of the government."

Terrorist threats are of two general kinds: those which announce that some action will be taken unless a certain terrorist demand is met and those which ostensibly serve as a warning of some action that has already been initiated. Both types of threats have the same political purpose, but they call for different responses. Careful analysis of the nature and content of each threat is necessary in order to determine an appropriate response. For example, the terrorist who threatens to kill hostages may or may not have the capability of carrying out his threat, but because the hostages are in his immediate power, the threat must be taken very seriously indeed. Whatever the tactical response decided upon, it must be predicated on the likelihood of the terrorist carrying out his threat unless it has been positively determined that he cannot. The terrorist who demands money to keep from detonating a bomb that he claims to have hidden in an unspecified place poses another type of problem. How serious is the risk that he is not bluffing? Clearly, the evidence has to be weighed in each individual case, but a serious responsibility rests on the shoulders of all who disregard such warnings. A specific warning that a bomb will explode in a crowded building in five minutes clearly calls for an immediate decision. Such a warning may represent a tactic in the War of Nerves or it may be part of a genuine terrorist plan to shift the responsibility for consequent harm onto the shoulders of the authorities concerned.

An understanding of the nature of such threats and warning, their purpose, and the overall strategy of the terrorist is important in determining the response. In addition, we need to develop a sound and practical threat analysis to guide those who must respond to many different manifestations of terrorism. In terms of legal response, threats that are part of a genuine terrorist campaign or War of Nerves—as distinct from mere mischievous imitation or psychopathological behavior—should be dealt with as seriously as the acts themselves.

INCIDENCE AND SEVERITY

The unsatisfactory nature of available data and the scattered, fragmentary nature of sources make it difficult to offer any firm estimates as to the incidence or severity of the different classes of terroristic activity described. Furthermore, because there is no agreement on definitions, data that might relate to true terroristic activity cannot be readily separated from that which has been categorized here as quasi-terroristic. Systematic collection of data about all types of terroristic activities on a nationwide scale has never been attempted. Efforts that have been made are limited in scope or have but recently commenced. Reports of bombings have only been systematically collected since 1969, and the data are not reliable before 1972. Information on hostage-taking incidents is not collected on a general basis and is not available in a form that would enable researchers to differentiate easily between incidents of a true terroristic nature and those which are quasi-terroristic.

Despite admittedly incomplete data, a number of useful observations can be made. Compared with other major countries of the West, the United States has not faced a serious political terrorist problem. True terrorism that has occurred has been almost exclusively domestic. It has been neither sustained nor effective, and must be considered limited or subrevolutionary in character. The United States has not experienced anything comparable to the bitter terroristic campaign of the IRA in England and Northern Ireland, nor has it been subjected to the type of terroristic activity engaged in by the Baader-Meinhof gang in the Federal Republic of Germany. Although there have been a number of assassinations and attempted assassinations of prominent political figures in this country, none has had the character of, for example, the killing of Spanish Premier Luis Carrero Blanco in Madrid in 1973. Political kidnapings that continue to take place in Central and South America, which are linked to an organized pattern of guerrilla warfare, have not touched off a rash of similar behavior here.

It would seem that the principal manifestation of true terrorism in the United States today is the bombing incident. Allowing for the vagaries of available data, study shows these to be substantially on the increase, and the quality of the devices and materials used reflects growing sophistication. In 1975, there were 2,053 bombing incidents, costing the lives of 69 persons, wounding 326 more, and causing property damage in excess of $26 million. Probably only about 83 of these bombings, however, were true terrorist bombings. With one or two notable exceptions, such as the bombing of Fraunces Tavern in New York City and the bombing at the La Guardia Airport, bombing attacks were mainly directed against property rather than at human life. There has been no indiscriminate, wanton killing by these means on a large scale, no resort to weapons of mass destruction, nor is there evidence of a systematic, coordinated terrorist campaign. Such political terrorism as does take place is of the protest type.

International terrorism has not been a matter of great concern to the United States within its own territories. This country has been spared tragic, terroristic acts like those which took lives at the airports of Paris, Rome, Athens, and Zurich. The United States was mainly spared, too, the pernicious letter bombing campaign that at one time assumed worldwide dimensions. Violent political groups, such as the Japanese Red Army, the Popular Front for the Liberation of Palestine, and the Provisional Wing of the IRA,

109

so far have not chosen the United States as a battleground. Foreign embassies and consulates have not been seized as they have in other countries, nor have murder and kidnaping of foreign nationals by domestic or international groups become a feature of the domestic scene. Although many aspects of United States foreign policy have been, from time to time, the subject of bitter controversy, no international terrorist campaign has been mounted for the purpose of effecting policy changes by violent means.

Unfortunately, United States citizens and interests overseas have suffered from international terrorism on a more serious scale. United States businesses in Latin American countries have been subjected to severe attack; their executives have been kidnaping victims whose ransoms have augmented the war chests of guerrilla groups. Attack on United States overseas investment has been part of the general strategy to bring about the conditions for revolution in some countries. During the period 1964 to 1974, 61 United States officials abroad were subjected to terrorist attacks, including 28 kidnapings. Fifteen of these officials were murdered. Substantial efforts toward protection of United States citizens and interests overseas have been taken both by the government and by the private sector.

Mindful of the events that have shaken the domestic peace in other countries, this country must take terrorist threats very seriously indeed. The tragic events that marred the 1972 Olympic Games in Munich have been ever-present to those responsible for the subsequent international sporting events. It would be irresponsible to ignore the possibility of threats to any major international event. Consequently, a great deal of tension and anticipation now surrounds such events, and even if fears do not materialize, the terrorists' purpose is well served. Although the overall impact of international terrorist activity has been quite small in terms of political effectiveness and even slighter in terms of actual human and material loss (between January 1968 and April 1974 there were 507 incidents, resulting in the deaths of 520 persons and 830 injuries), its effect upon general attitudes and preparedness has been considerable. International terrorists not only have succeeded in generating a climate of fear disproportionate of the material results of their endeavors, but also have caused considerable expenditure in anticipation of future threats. Spectacular terrorist successes overseas have not been lost on domestic terrorists, and there undoubtedly has been an element of contagion and imitation.

THE DISTINCTIVE CHARACTERISTICS OF MODERN TERRORISM

Terrorism as an instrument of political action is not new in form or substance. Read in a modern context, the declarations of the Russian anarchists of the last century — a fundamental expression of classical terrorism — have a strikingly modern ring to them. In all its forms, terrorism is a weapon of the weak against the strong; the terroristic technique is designed to redress in some measure the balance of power. The terrorist who takes hostages uses them as a bargaining counter — gambling that society's representatives will equate their value with the demands he has made. Although the terrorist is materially weaker than society in a situation of confrontation, his real strength lies in his own ruthlessness, recklessness, or the extent of his mental derangement. Thus, the single most important fact in determining a response to terrorism is to know how far the terrorist will go to attain his objectives. This ancient, unalterable element of terroristic strategy has a Catch-22 quality about it: any concession to the terrorist to save lives must be accounted a victory of sorts for him; any inflexibility leading to the loss of lives is, equally, a defeat for any but the most totalitarian society. Thus, modern terrorism exhibits all the basic elements of classical terrorism in their original form.

Nevertheless, there are several emerging characteristics that distinguish present-day terrorism. The first is a product of the technological vulnerability of modern society. The potential for harm to the services and institutions that supply society with its basic needs is greater today than ever before; society can be victimized with relatively little expenditure of effort and ingenuity by individuals or by small groups. A single individual, with comparatively unsophisticated weaponry, little advance planning, no special skills, and little intelligence, can take over a modern airliner and for a brief time control expensive property and human lives. This fact alone has substantially increased the bargaining power of the modern terrorist; nation states are forced, when their most vital and vulnerable interests are threatened, into bargaining parity with the terrorist. Even governments professing inflexible policies are often beaten into a posture of submission when their international relations are jeopardized by terrorist action. This has proved distasteful and humiliating for some, but it must be accepted and dealt with realistically. Through the power of terrorism, the individual has come into his own once more. As Richard Clutterbuck has pointed out [30]:

The circumstances of the new war resemble ancient times when battles could be decided by single combat. The spectacular killing or capture of one individual can strike terror into the hearts of a million others. A capitulation to blackmail or ransom can inspire other terrorist groups, and can erode the confidence of civilized communities throughout the world.

Modern terrorism has been assisted by developments in intercontinental travel and mass communications. Terrorists now move easily and with considerable speed across continents. There is substantial evidence of technology transfer, training, and even combined operations among terrorist groups of differing organization and purpose. Most frightening of all, perhaps, is the fact that acts of extraordinary violence have come to serve as a form of mass entertainment. Acts of terrorism have gained immediacy and diffusion through television, which conveys the terrorist message to millions worldwide. The modern terrorist has been quick to exploit this advantage; he has become a master of the medium in a way that shows government as a poor rival. Formerly, in countries where free speech and communication were jealously guarded rights, it would have been unthinkable for violent subversives to have seized control of the organs of mass communication. Today, this is a commonplace consequence of terrorist action. In many ways, the modern terrorist is the very creation of the mass media. He has been magnified, enlarged beyond his own powers by others.

The modern terrorist wields power far in excess of anything his predecessors could have imagined. Today, all must pause before the awesome consequences of possible terrorist action. In former times, terrorist victims might have been counted in hundreds at most: now their numbers could reach to hundreds of thousands. New technologies have placed within easy reach of the modern terrorist, who has the weapons of mass destruction, the ability to create terrifying, uncontrollable, and irreversible situations. For most political terrorists, destruction is only contemplated as a prelude to reconstruction, however unspecific. Once begun, modern destruction could preclude any possibility of reconstruction. So far, few terrorists have displayed such frankly suicidal qualities. The modern political terrorist does not feel that he is fighting for a hopeless cause; by and large, his aim is political legitimacy through the selective use of violence. Most terrorists are not solipsists; they are conscious of their place in a world they are anxious to change or control by their violence. The political implications of their acts have to be considered carefully by terrorists: the deaths of too many innocents could result in alienation rather than intimidation. Perhaps, because the potential gain is greater and the ready means more powerful, the constraints upon the modern, political terrorist are stronger than ever.

THE CHANGING FACE OF INTERNATIONAL TERRORISM

Since the early 1950's, military strategists have been trying to resolve the problem of mankind's potential for mass destruction. Nuclear power has made all-out war between great nations an unrealistic proposition, but some form of limited warfare appears to be necessary in the regulation of international relationships. This development has had profound implications for international terrorism, particularly as to wars of national liberation and the struggles for political self-determination. These age-old sentiments have been and are being exploited in a way that was neither desirable nor possible in former times. Many nations have recognized the great potential of terrorism; the terrorist is now the spearhead of a developing theory and practice of surrogate warfare. Governments unwilling to risk the consequences of conventional warfare to alter the present balance of power more and more are subsidizing, training, and deploying clandestine organizations ranging from unofficial, quasi-armies to small, anarchical terrorist groups.

Of itself, this is hardly an original development in world affairs, but the realities of the nuclear age and the present uneasy balance of power suggest that more of the technology and resources of some nations will support vicious, desperate terrorists whose mission is to create terror for carefully designed, coercive purposes. They will be employed to provoke incidents and create panic and chaos in an adversary's territory, weaken its resolve to resist or defend its interests, damage its ability to provide vital services for its people, and force it to expend resources for internal defense to a damaging extent. Terrorism is an extremely cheap means to such ends. Sponsorship greatly facilitates the terrorist's work and enhances his prospects of success. Transnational terrorists sponsored in this way have the benefit of permanent safe havens and operational bases. They are equipped with sophisticated weaponry and ample economic and material resources, making unofficial technology transfer and cooperation among established terrorist groups largely unnecessary.

Terrorists enjoying the sponsorship of a nation state will generally be aiming at some form of political legitimacy; while they are seeking to attain it, many innocents will perish at the hands of criminal groups clandestinely supported by many of the governments that have frustrated the international cooperation necessary to the control of this menace. So far, the efforts of such terrorists have not been directed at the United States or its interests, but this country ought properly to regard itself as the ultimate target of such groups. This relatively new development should not go unnoticed; proper steps to meet the threat should be taken. United States foreign policy should mark this country's disapproval of nations sponsoring terrorist organizations and cooperate with like-minded members of the international community in this opposition.

THE HISTORICAL NATURE OF TERRORISM AND MASS VIOLENCE IN THE UNITED STATES

Episodes of extreme violence have occurred with depressing regularity throughout the two-hundred-year history of the United States. The level of civil violence tolerated in the United States belies the stability of the country's social and political structures. This facet of American society is encapsulated in H. Rap Brown's famous epigram that violence is necessary and as American as cherry pie. American industrial relations, in particular, have been marked by violent, bloody struggles. Ethnic and religious strife also have led to intense violence and today give the impression of unresolved tension lurking behind an apparent calm.

All too often commissions of inquiry have been asked to answer the question: "Why have atrocious things occurred to interrupt the domestic tranquillity of our Republic?" [*Riots, Civil and Criminal Disorders,* Part 16, p. 2976.] Mass violence has generally been spontaneous and unorganized; most inquiries have sought unsuccessfully to find foreign influences at work. Deep-seated antagonisms have exploded in a dramatic way, but more often than not the violence has subsided as rapidly as it began. In the past, while some areas of the country were experiencing grave disturbances of the public order, others continued tranquil, orderly development. The size of the country and the pluralistic nature of American society account in part for the Nation's capacity to absorb a high level of domestic violence. With the notable exception of the Civil War, no episode of extreme violence has ever seriously threatened the viability of the Republic or the functioning of its institutions. This is, perhaps, the most significant fact about mass violence in the United States—

one that distinguishes it from countries experiencing comparable levels of domestic violence.

Scattered episodes of political terrorism have occurred regularly and continue to occur in the United States, but they have been of a subrevolutionary or limited type. The size of the country, the decentralization of power, and the nature of American social and political organization may have proved too daunting for those with revolutionary objectives. The fragmentary nature of the terroristic effort and the lack of cohesiveness among the different terrorist groups have limited American terrorism to an overall purposelessness. While at times an ugly local phenomenon that has taken lives, damaged property, and generated great fear, terrorism has never seriously disturbed the domestic tranquillity. Perhaps the most serious terrorist episode in our history occurred in 1919 and 1920. The years following the end of World War I generated a fear among Americans that occasionally reached almost hysterical proportions. The Wall Street bombing in 1920, following upon the Red Scare of 1919, and the consequent Palmer Raids, mark the watershed of American political terrorism. American political terrorists have never captured public sympathy or produced fear that inhibited government response. There has been little prospect that American terrorism would develop into an advanced stage of guerrilla warfare. Thus, the writings and declarations of modern terrorist groups, such as the Weather Underground, ultimately take on an unrealistic tone. The emergence of the intellectual terrorists of the 1960's and 1970's has led some to visualize domestic terrorism in proportions quite out of keeping with the American tradition. American terrorism and quasi-terrorism have always been most dangerous when conducted in limited terms and with limited objectives, such as the violent actions of the Puerto Rican liberation movement. Although the United States cannot be expected to remain wholly untouched by new and powerful developments in modern terrorism, the American experience does not suggest that terrorists having more ambitious aims are likely to be more successful than their predecessors.

AMERICAN TERRORISM AND MASS VIOLENCE IN A COMPARATIVE CONTEXT

During the past few years, terrorism has come to occupy an increasingly important place in public attention worldwide. The spectacular nature of terrorist activities assures comprehensive news coverage; modern communications make each incident an international event. An incident such as the Munich Olympic tragedy was a grave warning to other countries and a direct stimulus to establish countermeasures. Such events become permanent landmarks in the history of terrorism and mass violence against which subsequent incidents can be measured. Although terrorism, in cause and manifestation, differs widely from country to country, it is useful to compare the situation of the United States with other countries. The United States experience is an integral part of the contemporary pattern of modern mass violence, and developments, characteristics, and incidents elsewhere are important factors in detecting the trends of mass disorders in this country and in designing responses to them.

From a comparative point of view, certain manifestations of international terrorism are more interesting and relevant than others. The experience of the United Kingdom with the terrorism of the IRA is the product of a political antagonism that has no counterpart in this country. Although interesting and instructive in the matter of responses, this situation does not suggest likely developments in the United States. The Spanish experience, too, is based upon stresses and tensions peculiar to that country's political life. On the other hand, there are countries whose experience with terrorism—although the product of social and political conditions dissimilar to those in the United States—is worthy of extended consideration. Of such interest are the experiences of Latin American countries—partly because of their proximity to the United States, partly because of the extent of United States involvement in those countries, but especially because United States interests are often the target of native terrorism.

Political terrorism is a fact of life in international politics. United States involvement in international affairs inevitably exposes the country's interests to terrorist activity. Conventional, international relations increasingly have become a target of terrorist activity. So much transnational terrorist activity is related to national or ideological causes that every political movement is of potential interest to those concerned with terrorism in the United States. The frequency and severity of international terrorist incidents is directly related to the social and political circumstances out of which they develop. Thus, where a nationalist movement is engaged in a war of liberation, such as the Algerian FLN struggle against France, terrorist incidents are daily occurrences and constitute a continual threat to the domestic tranquillity. Similarly, the conflict in Northern Ireland is part of an overall struggle whether the issue is seen in terms of self-determination or the conservation of entrenched rights. A very high percentage of the world's terrorism since the end of World War II can be described in these terms and has come to be expected, tolerated, or suffered in the same way as war itself. Such terrorism takes on international significance when the struggle spills over into noncombatant territory or when terrorists deliberately seek to involve a neutral power to draw attention to their cause or stimulate international action. Terrorism as a function of internal strife cannot fail to have an international import. As has been said: "[Although] the causes of civil strife most often are found in the political and social structure of the disrupted state, the outcome of that strife very frequently has a profound influence on the allocation of power in the world community." [John C. Novogrod, "Internal Strife, Self-Determination and World Order," in *International Terrorism and Political Crimes,* pp. 98-99.]

When the manifestations of internal strife keep within national boundaries, reactions to them on diplomatic and other levels can take place through conventional channels. However, the terrorist has no cause to respect these limitations, and a distinct feature of modern, international terrorism is the calculated involvement of foreign interests and foreign governments by means of terroristic acts. Foreign diplomats and businessmen have been seized and ransomed for political purposes; foreign embassies and consulates have been violated frequently in order to affect the normal course of international relations. Modern transnational terrorism is designed to coerce governments that can in turn bring pressure on the true adversary, and the instant victim becomes an unwilling participant. The Munich incident was directed at Israel, though it took place on West German soil. Croatian terrorists, adversaries of the Yugoslav government, have made Sweden a battleground, assassinating the Yugoslav Ambassador there, seizing a consulate, and attacking Swedish aircraft. The United States Ambassador and Consul-General to Haiti were kidnaped and held hostage in order to pressure the Haitian government into releasing political prisoners. A review of international terrorist incidents of the past 10 years shows increasing use of such activity as a form of armed diplomacy.

International terrorists may be broadly classified as minority nationalist groups, Marxist revolutionary groups, anarchist groups, neo-Fascist and extreme rightwing groups, and ideological mercenaries. National liberation movements show considerable organization, with long-term planning and well-defined objectives. Generally, they receive support from private sympathizers and encouragement, training, materials, and occasional safe haven from sympathetic governments. There is considerable evidence that terrorists are receiving systematic training in Cuba, the Soviet Union, and Eastern Bloc countries. These terrorists have been employed mainly where guerrilla warfare is ostensibly being waged to overthrow a legitimate government, but they are obviously available for attacks against other targets. The existence of such terrorist organizations poses a grave threat not only to persons and property, but also to international relations.

Different styles of response to terrorist action are also of comparative interest. Antiterrorist policies are mainly determined by the politics and philosophies of the systems in question. There are hardline approaches, such as that taken by Spain, whose severe antiterrorist laws are enforced with considerable rigor despite substantial international disapproval. The other extreme is represented by Austria, which has repeatedly capitulated to terrorist demands, with the expressed objective of saving human lives. Although this policy may have affected Austria's international relations, it does not seem to have given substantial encouragement to terrorists. The Federal Republic of Germany and its interests have been frequent targets of terroristic action both at home and in other countries; the country's willingness to accede to terrorist demands, particularly the death of the West German Ambassador to Guatemala, may have encouraged subsequent terrorist action. There has been a definite hardening of West German attitudes in recent months. The government has taken more sophisticated antiterrorist measures, and new antiterrorist laws have been passed. These actions and the resolute prosecution of the Baader-Meinhof gang may have reversed the trend. The Netherlands, which has an extremely liberal criminal policy, has followed a much harder line with terrorists because of recent experiences. This policy seems to have had some deterrent effect.

A number of European countries, including the United Kingdom, the Federal Republic of Germany, Sweden, and Spain have found it necessary to enact special antiterrorist laws. The antiterrorist law of the United Kingdom, largely a response to IRA terrorism, gives broad powers to law enforcement. Neither the Federal Republic of Germany nor the United Kingdom, both of which have been subject to extreme terrorist attacks, have a death penalty. The United Kingdom strongly resisted an attempt to reintroduce the death penalty for terrorists following a particularly severe wave of terrorist bombings in 1974. Most West European countries respond to mass violence and terrorism on a quasi-military basis, with specialist units trained and available for the purpose. Rapid communications and the small size of these countries facilitate such a response. Law enforcement reorganization, particularly in the Federal Republic of Germany, has improved the antiterrorist response. Latin American countries — Brazil, Argentina, and Uruguay in particular — have been forced into a strictly military response that has been broadly successful in denying terrorists the political advantages they seek. The Brazilian and Uruguayan responses have been particularly effective in breaking up terrorist organizations, but at an enormous expense to civil liberties.

Although attitudes toward negotiations with terrorists differ, it can be said that no nation holds fast to a no-negotiation policy when its vital interests are at stake. The official United States policy is not to pay ransom or accede to terrorist blackmail. This clearly does not preclude negotiations, and the United States always will do whatever it can to obtain the release of hostages. An inflexible approach is often unrealistic, and when this attitude receives publicity, may well prejudice a reasonable outcome. The United States position was criticized following the death of the United States Ambassador to the Sudan, who had been taken hostage by members of the Black September organization. Israel follows an extremely hard line in negotiations with all terrorists, but has, on occasion, made concessions, particularly when international relations have been jeopardized. Spain, which pursues a very hard line with domestic terrorists, has adopted a more moderate approach when protected members of the international community in Spain have suffered at the hands of terrorists.

Many countries, notably the United Kingdom, have opted for extensive prolongation of hostage situations together with a firm policy of offering no important concessions, when a terrorist confrontation with authority has been stabilized. This approach was adopted by the Eirean authorities when Dutch businessman Tiede Herrema was kidnaped and by the Netherlands authorities when South Moluccan terrorists hijacked a train and occupied the Indonesian consulate. The success of this pragmatic approach depends to a large extent upon the pressures that the terrorists can bring to bear upon the actual situation or elsewhere. For example, the United Kingdom showed its readiness to make appropriate concessions to prevent further violence when Lebanese skyjacker Leila Khaled was released as part of a concerted international effort to free passengers held by members of the Popular Front for the Liberation of Palestine.

Two important features of international terrorist negotiation emerge from this analysis. First, the position of the nation states engaged in bargaining with terrorists generally has been extremely flexible, but there have been clearly understood limits to the demands that would be met. Nonnegotiable matters vary from country to country and reflect national priorities. Terrorists have responded realistically to this position and generally have settled for much less than they had originally demanded. Second, there has been a marked disinclination, even on the part of the most determined terrorist groups, to carry a situation to its ultimate limits. Few terrorists have been willing to die rather than accept defeat. This fact has important implications for the design of responses.

Many international hostage negotiations have required the intervention of neutral, usually diplomatic, third-party intermediaries. Such interventions, designed to resolve the matter satisfactorily for all parties, often alter or supersede ordinary contingency plans and command functions. Most countries have accepted this interference with national sovereignty on the premise that it leads to a speedier resolution of the matter.

THE COSTS OF TERRORISM AND MASS VIOLENCE

In the absence of reliable data, it is impossible to offer even a general estimate of the economic costs of extraordinary violence. Given the unpredictable nature of terrorism, the problem is similar to quantifying the effects of natural disasters, and as such is an unrealistic exercise. The economic cost of a major urban riot can be roughly assessed in terms of property destroyed and funds expended to restore order, to reestablish the community's normal functioning, and to make good the damage. (See, for example the interesting tables contained in *Riots, Civil and Criminal Disorders.*) But even the actual costs of civil disturbances are largely of historic interest and offer no real guidance for estimating the cost of future disturbances, which could assume quite different forms and dimensions.

The material losses involved in the terrorist hijacking and

destruction of one commercial jet airliner run into millions of dollars The insurance costs of the Middle East skyjackings to Jordan and Cairo in 1970 were about $55 million; by comparison, the $26 million in losses attributable to domestic terrorist activity in the United States during 1975 seems small. Political kidnapings in Latin America have reaped a rich reward, mainly from United States business interests; ransom in one case has risen to almost $60 million. Authorities in these countries are justly concerned, knowing that ransom and protection money is building terrorist strength while their own defense budgets remain limited. Many foreign businesses in Latin America can only continue to operate by paying terrorists the equivalent of protection money. This cost is passed on to the consumer in the form of increased prices. Added to these direct costs are those incurred by individuals, corporations, and society generally in maintaining a minimum state of preparedness against future terrorist action. When all these sums are taken into account, we can grossly estimate the dimension of the economic burden that the community must assume as a result of terrorism.

The psychological costs of terrorism are even more difficult to estimate. The intensity of terrorist campaigns varies considerably, but a War of Nerves can be as costly in the long run as a campaign designed to inflict material losses. Terrorist activity can substantially lower the quality of life in a community, alter the attitudes and habits of the people exposed to its dangers, and make normal functioning difficult or impossible. Terrorism can give rise to a siege mentality, especially among those directly threatened as targets, and can interfere substantially with the normal human contacts to which members of a free society are accustomed. What has been called "an acute situational state" has been reported from Belfast, Northern Ireland. "[Patients], usually women and children were weeping, trembling uncontrollably and couldn't remember either their names or where they lived. They were often unable to speak and sometimes these symptoms did not immediately respond to a mild dosage of sedatives. According to the report, these symptoms result from living in an atmosphere of constant terror where the enemy is not easily identifiable and violence is blind and arbitrary." [*Science Digest,* September 1973, p. 26.]

The overall cost of terrorism in this respect must not be exaggerated. For all its spectacular exhibitions, terrorism affects comparatively few people. The United States has learned to live with what once would have been regarded as an intolerably high level of violent crime; the total of all terrorist incidents pales in effect when compared to the 20,000 criminal homicides committed in this country in 1974. Even in a city like Belfast, life does not come to a standstill under the terrorist menace. People learn to adapt even to the most intensive anxiety-producing conditions.

Fear of terrorist victimization is not great in the United States, and the incidence of terrorist attacks would have to rise very substantially, even in selective fashion, to generate a climate of real fear. The psychological burden of terrorism is probably greatest for prominent public officials, but the assassinations of recent years, although they have led to greatly increased precautions, do not appear to have deterred candidates from seeking the highest public offices. United States businessmen overseas have been advised to take suitable precautions for their safety, but they have not been driven from the market by psychological warfare.

The social costs of terrorism and mass violence are incalculable as well. Violence constitutes an insidious form of social indoctrination. It has been said that: "In violent crime man becomes a wolf to man, threatening or destroying the personal safety of his victim in a terrifying act. Violent crime (particularly street crime) engenders fear—the deepseated fear of the hunted in the presence of the hunter. Today this fear is gnawing at the vitals of urban America." [Platt, p. 409.] A society cannot live happily under the shadow of terror any more than it can live easily amid the constant threat of social upheaval. The political terrorist seeks to generate unrest that he can exploit; his acts have a seminal quality. The Weather Underground has announced, "We create the seeds of the new society in the struggle for the destruction of the empire.''

The social unrest caused by mass violence also is contagious. Hans Toch has written [p. 203]:

One reason why violence comes so easy to rioters is that they can derive it from a common cause. They can see themselves individually laboring toward group ends. They can feel themselves partners of a joint enterprise. They can conceive of their own acts as defined and sanctioned by a larger effort. Every solitary marauder can come to regard himself as a member of a crusade.

Mass disorders challenge established authority and the stability of social life; they create uncertainty and tension. Their violence breeds suspicion and divisiveness, particularly when it is racially motivated. In fact, violent crime is but a relatively small proportion of all crime, and terroristic crime, a smaller part of that. Yet it has a disproportionate influence upon the lives and thought of people and the priorities and energies they devote to responding to it. Growth and domestic prosperity depend to a large extent upon the sense of security provided by sound government enjoying a proper measure of popular support. In our major urban centers, the source and repository of so much American wealth, much of this security has been eroded by a pervasive sense of violence. The true cost of terrorism and mass violence, in social terms, is to be found in the diminished quality of social life and interaction.

Political terrorism is the spearhead of attack upon established political systems. It is directed at destroying political figures and institutions, weakening the confidence of the people in the political system, creating confusion and disorder, and provoking massive repression that diminishes the fundamental freedoms enjoyed by citizens. Political violence is a form of vicious intimidation wholly antithetical to the democratic system. Gurr notes that [p. 3]: ''[Since] 1945, violent attempts to overthrow governments have been more common than national elections.'' The political costs of terrorism and mass violence are potentially great in terms of the distortion of the system, the disruption of its regular processes, and the divorce of the people from its organs of government.

Those who seek political control by extralegal means frequently resort to street violence and terrorism. We are reminded that: "[The] SA [The Sturmabteilung, or German "Brownshirt" Movement] was employed as a terroristic group, in order to gain for the Nazis possession and control of the streets. That is another way of saying that it was a function of the SA to beat up and terrorize all political opponents . . . 'possession of the streets is the key to power in the State — for this reason the SA marched and fought. The public would never have received knowledge of the agitative speeches of the little Reichstag faction and its propagandists or of the desires and aims of the Party if the martial tread and battlesong of the SA companies had not beat the measures for the truth of a relentless criticism of the state of affairs in the governmental system.' " [*Trial of the Major War Criminals Before the International Military Tribunal,* Proceedings, Vol. IV, p. 134.] It is but a short step from such general intimidation to selective assassination of political opponents.

Terrorist assassinations of political leaders generally have not had significant political impact. The nature of the American political system does not hold out the prospect of great political change as a result of selective, political assassination. Although four Presidents of the United States have been assassinated and attempts upon and threats to the lives of others have been made, the effects on government as such have been slight. A more massive onslaught, such as that threatened by some domestic terrorist groups, would have to be taken very seriously indeed in terms of its political consequences. Unquestionably, such acts and threats have had a marked effect upon the precautions that have had to be taken to protect officeholders and candidates alike. The sight of numerous, alert bodyguards physically restraining the President of the United States, though necessary today, is not a dignified spectacle. The Presidency has been driven into a position of increasing defensiveness and impersonality as a result of assassination threats; it is too dangerous to allow Presidents and even presidential candidates to roam freely among the people. Although in a time of effective mass communications this probably has little political effect, the symbolic consequences are considerable and represent an undeniable victory for the protagonists of political violence.

On another symbolic level, the consequences of political assassination can be far-reaching also. The traumas of the assassinations of President John F. Kennedy and Senator Robert F. Kennedy are with us still. It has been said that, "Anger, fear, shock, hopelessness, loss, and sadness were overwhelming reactions." [Kirkham, Levy, and Crotty, p. 107.] The reactions to the murder of Dr. Martin Luther King, Jr., were violent and destructive and undeniably put back the cause for which Dr. King had worked so long. The political costs of extreme violence must, therefore, be estimated on at least two levels: the direct costs of the response to it, which can be assessed with some accuracy, and the emotional or symbolic costs, which cannot. Both are costs the Nation can ill afford; both are interrelated with the other costs of which mention has been made.

FUTURE TRENDS IN TERRORISM AND MASS VIOLENCE

A majority of experts predicts an eventual increase in terroristic activity and an escalation of its intensity. At this time, the incidence of terrorism seems to have reached a temporary plateau. Events of recent years suggest, for the immediate future, no more than its regular, albeit disquieting, growth subject to the influence of social and political factors. Conditions in the United States do not seem to indicate a massive expansion of terroristic activity, any radical change in its nature, or its extension into a form of guerrilla warfare. Any expansion that takes place is likely to be in the area of covert terrorism, and, except for aberrant cases, massive, direct confrontation with the authorities is not likely to occur. What is likely to increase is the intensity of the terroristic activity in terms of employment of sophisticated modern technology. This will involve many leaps in the dark for the terrorist, and responses to it will be predicated upon equal uncertainty.

For some, terrorism has become a way of life, and as long as the major international issues remain unresolved, such activity will be, for many, the only way of reacting to the frustrations and perceived inequities. Terrorism is contagious; successes and new developments in one part of the world are likely to attract ready imitators in another. It is probable that sponsored terrorism as surrogate warfare will increase. It is difficult to imagine a situation that would produce a substantial measure of international agreement to curb terrorism; however, the growing menace will lead to more international cooperation, particularly the exchange of information, among countries with common interests. Although international cooperation must be encouraged, most countries should look to their own resources as the most effective means of defense.

Because terrorism does not follow a discernible pattern, it is difficult to identify future trends in terroristic activity. The most dreadful possibilities have not been realized, but they remain and must be faced realistically. It is possible that increased awareness, increasing sophistication of responses, and the precautionary measures that have been taken already are having an inhibiting effect on terroristic activity. The most dangerous terrorists are those who have no allegiance to any realizable cause. These persons—whether seriously deranged or simply nihilistic—are very few in number but extremely hard to contain. No form of response to their actions is likely to have any deterrent value. Although no security system can ever attain perfection, preventive measures clearly are worthwhile, especially where the possibility of deterrence is minimal. As a general prescription, society should aim to outwit the terrorist rather than to outfight him.

Civil disturbances, on the other hand, seem to be cyclical. Generally, they are the product of local social and political conditions. Although they can be exacerbated by outside influences, disorders are rarely engendered by them. Extensive external interference in American civil disturbances is extremely unlikely in the near future, although extremist terrorist groups may well take advantage of mass disorders for their own purposes. It is important to remember that some of the most serious episodes of mass violence in this country have been touched off by relatively insignificant incidents. The mood of the community should be monitored constantly; signs of impending violence never should be ignored. Contingency planning should be predicated on the assumption that a deep well of violence underlies the apparent calm and stability of the American social scene. We must be especially careful during periods of rising expectations, particularly when these cannot be satisfied so fully and expeditiously as the disadvantaged might desire. Labor unrest, racial violence, and poverty are all issues that can lead once again to civil disorder. It is all too easy in times of relative calm to ignore the underlying causes of mass violence; only the near certainty of its recrudescence serves as a reminder and stimulus to the preventive action that should be taken.

REFERENCES

1. Arendt, Hannah. *On Violence.* New York: Harcourt, Brace, and World, Inc., 1969.

2. Bassiouni, M. Cherif, ed. *International Terrorism and Political Crimes.* Springfield, Ill.: Charles C. Thomas, 1975.

3. Bowyer Bell, J. *Transnational Terror.* Washington, D.C.: American Enterprise Institute for Public Policy Research, 1975.

4. Clutterbuck, Richard. *Living with Terrorism.* London: Faber & Faber, 1975.

5. Davies, James Downing, ed. *When Men Revolt and Why.* New York: The Free Press, 1971.

6. Gurr, Ted R. *Why Men Rebel.* Princeton, N.J.: Princeton University Press, 1970.

7. Hofstadter, Richard, and Michael Wallace, eds. *American Violence: Documentary History.* New York: Vintage Books, 1971.

8. Kirkham, James F., Sheldon G. Levy, and William J. Crotty. *Assassination and Political Violence: A Staff Report to the National Commission on the Causes and Prevention of Violence.* New York: Bantam Books, 1970.

9. Marighella, Carlos. *Minimanual of the Urban Guerrilla.* Havana, Cuba: Tricontinental, 1970.

10. Platt, Anthony M. *The Politics of Riot Commissions.* New York: Collier Books, 1971.

11. *Report of the National Advisory Commission on Civil Disorders,* Washington, D.C.: Government Printing Office, 1968.

12. *Riots, Civil and Criminal Disorders,* Hearings Before the Permanent Subcommittee on Investigations of the Committee on Government Operations, U.S. Senate, Washington, D.C.: Government Printing Office, 1967.

13. Schwarzenberger, Georg. "Terrorists, Guerrilleros and Mercenaries," *Toledo Law Review,* Fall/Winter, 1971, pp. 71-88.

14. Toch, Hans. *Violent Men.* Chicago: Aldine Publishing Company, 1969.

15. *Trial of the Major War Criminals Before the Interna-*

tional Military Tribunal, Proceedings, Vol. IV. Nuremburg, 1947.

16. United Nations, Report of the Ad Hoc Committee on International Terrorism, General Assembly Official Records: 28th Session, Supplement No. 28 [A-9028].

17. Van Den Haag, Ernest. *Political Violence and Civil Disobedience.* New York: Harper Torch Books, 1972.

18. Wilkinson, Paul. *Political Terrorism.* London: Macmillan Press Limited, 1974.

19. Wilson, Jerry V. *Police Report.* Boston: Little, Brown and Company, 1975.

STANDARD 9.5

HANDLING OF JUVENILE OFFENDERS

Juveniles incarcerated for acts of terrorism and political violence should not be confined in adult institutions, save as an exceptional measure, nor be treated as adult offenders. Juvenile offenders should be given the treatment appropriate to their status and condition in secure institutions that meet the general criteria recommended for the confinement of this type of offender.

COMMENTARY

Juveniles as a class show a marked propensity for individual and group violence. Juveniles tend, also, to be more impressionable than adults and more susceptible to current fads and influences of all kinds. The modern juvenile has a sophistication and awareness born of the pervasiveness of present-day communications. Today's youth is keenly aware not only of trends in criminal justice but also of their possible impact on his own life style and activities. A recent *Philadelphia Inquirer* article on teenage gangs [Dec. 21, 1975] indicates that "Contrary to views held by many, trends in criminal sentencing are well understood on the streets." The same article convincingly documents the manner in which these trends have helped shape delinquent behavior among members of these juvenile gangs.

Juveniles have indulged in a significant amount of violent, cruel, and wanton criminal behavior, much of which could be characterized as terroristic. Juveniles account for almost half the arrests for serious crimes in the United States today, and a very high percentage of all violent crime is committed by members of this age group. In the main, juvenile terroristic activity has manifested itself through organized street gangs, many of which have been responsible for creating a substantial climate of fear in urban areas and have, on occasion, fought pitched battles that resulted in the killing of both rival gang members and innocent bystanders. Many of these gangs are ethnic in character, and their organization and influence are such that they have considerable impact of a semipolitical character. Sometimes their influence extends well beyond the geographic confines of their operations, particularly into institutions where members or ex-members are incarcerated, and transcends the boundaries of both age and race.

Over the years, while retaining their potential for violence, some of these gangs have developed into national radical organizations of some political and social sophistication. Prominent among these is the Young Lords Party, a revolutionary group composed principally of Puerto Rican youth. It began as a street gang in the slums in 1969 and was known originally as the Young Lords Organization, with branches in New York and Chicago. The organization was active in Attica before the uprising, and has now achieved a considerable institutional following with contacts with other radical groups across the country. These developments have considerable potential for the extension of terrorism and other forms of political violence. Although to date there has been little evidence of a substantial incursion of juveniles into the field of organized political violence and terrorism, either by way of imitation or initiation, this possibility should not be overlooked, particularly in the light of international experience with the use of children of quite tender years as "freedom fighters." While it is probable that certain groups would avoid using juveniles for acts of terrorism, on account of their presumed immaturity and unreliability, the eventuality of their involvement should not be discounted. The more lenient treatment generally accorded the juvenile offender and the willingness of youth to engage, with typical irresponsibility, in enterprises of this sort make their use attractive to terrorist leaders.

The correctional management and treatment of the juvenile poses special philosophical and practical problems, and the violent juvenile offender is a matter for particular concern. One of the most disturbing developments of recent years has been the emergence of the violent, alienated juvenile whose early entry on a criminal career gives rise to special preventive and remedial difficulties. This standard recognizes the peculiar problems posed by juvenile offenders and the inappropriateness of applying to them methods designed for the control and treatment of the adult offender. It is to be hoped that, notwithstanding the depravity of the deed, the juvenile who commits acts of terrorism and political violence will be more amenable to treatment and offer a better prospect of rehabilitation than an adult offender. There is a real need for the special correctional problems of the juvenile who has committed acts of terrorism and political violence to be handled in an appropriate setting. There are sound reasons why such an offender cannot be treated like a mature adult; the commission of such acts, however serious, at an early age should not become an excuse for consigning him to an institutional regimen likely to confirm him in his criminal career; nor should it be taken as an indication of the hopelessness of his return to open society. Although the potential for dangerous behavior on the part of juveniles is no less and may even be greater than that presented by the adult offender, the fear generated by their acts and the social repudiation of their conduct ought not to blind us to the need for treatment of a very different order and in a very different setting from those appropriate in the case of an adult. While the type of terror in which juveniles have commonly engaged is often wanton, indiscriminate, and lacking in feeling for the victim, it can usually be seen, by reason of the character of the actors, to have a quality significantly distinct from the terrorism purposefully engaged in by adult groups.

The commission of an adult crime does not make a juvenile an adult. A juvenile who commits an act of terrorism may merit the label "terrorist," but he does not cease, on that account, to be a juvenile. He ought, in consequence, to be treated as a juvenile, albeit one who has committed a serious crime. This standard recommends that he be so treated and processed, being sent for treatment to an institution suitable for his care, control, and custody.

REFERENCES

1. Gerard, Roy. "Institutional Innovations in Juvenile Corrections," *Federal Probation,* December 1970.

2. National Advisory Commission on Criminal Justice Standards and Goals: *Corrections.* Washington, D.C.: Government Printing Office, 1973.

3. Wicks, Robert J. *Correctional Psychology.* New York: Harper and Row, 1974.

SUMMARY

In summarizing, I have chosen to define terrorism as an aggregate social behavior, which manifests itself in the following ways: political anarchy, prison gangs, street gangs, and outlaw motorcycle gangs. Recalling the earlier discussion of terrorism, one must firmly understand that terrorism is an act or threat of an act for purposes of instilling in the victim anxiousness and fear through coercion. Gang organizational structure in its most fundamental form must include the following: antisocial behavior, most often exhibited by criminality, the dynamics of projection and a cause which is non-utilitarian, malicious and seemingly spontaneous. In its purest form the behavior would include sophisticated covert activity, classic guerrilla warfare and predetermined strategy.

Let us now turn to the etiology of terrorism and gang crime. The major causal factor is immature and inappropriate behavior coupled with an attempt to overcome unrealistic social barriers. The outgrowth is a result of interpersonal dynamics. Conventional norms, values and mores are cast aside as a person's support for social order dissipates. This support is literally transcended into hatred for conventional society, politically and socially. The actor begins a deliberate recruitment strategy to seek out those who think like him. A process then occurs which involves motivation, training and organization of this sub-cultural group. They begin to act out their group philosophy, which offends the sentiments of probity and pity in the remaining majority of society.

As this social disorganizational process occurs on a continuum, both deviant and criminal behavior are acted out. Additionally, by peer pressure, a constant bombardment of the imposition of gang values, along with control of the gang by coercion from within, a total loss of social reality occurs. It is at this juncture that the actors gravitate towards malicious and destructive activity in a most fanatical way.

Finally, as a result of the role dispossession of terrorists and gang members, they literally become a new person, hostile to nearly all of society with no constructive idea as to how they would substitute for the inequities they have perceived in society. Their inability to re-acculturate leaves no alternative for them but to remain on the periphery of society.

As with all social problems, the first step toward combating terrorism and gang crime is awareness, an attitude toward becoming pro-active or preventative, instead of merely reactive. It is important to maintain external social order which, contrary to public opinion and legislation, must include a stepped-up intelligence effort on the part of public safety agencies for the benefit of the public and not to the public's detriment. Intervention must continue to include negotiations between social order agencies and the violent actors.

As for the general public, knowledge of these groups and an understanding of one's own vulnerability to victimization by these groups serve to promote a responsive collective social action. And, in the final analysis, an undesirable social condition can only be ameliorated by collective social action. Until we deal with the problems of permissive legislation, poor judicial procedure and intolerable social conditions, there can be no optimistic prognosis.

THE END